S0-BJB-694

SEX DIFFERENCES AND LEARNING

GARLAND BIBLIOGRAPHIES IN
CONTEMPORARY EDUCATION
(VOL. 11)

GARLAND REFERENCE LIBRARY
OF SOCIAL SCIENCE
(VOL. 418)

THE GARLAND BIBLIOGRAPHIES IN CONTEMPORARY EDUCATION

Advisory Editor:
Joseph M. McCarthy

1. *Issues in Adult Basic Education*
   by Darlene Russ-Eft, David P. Rubin, and Rachel E. Holmen
2. *Contemporary Approaches to Moral Education*
   by James Leming
3. *Teacher Effectiveness*
   by Marjorie Powell and Joseph W. Beard
4. *Higher Education Finance*
   by Edward R. Hines and John R. McCarthy
5. *Teacher Attitudes*
   by Marjorie Powell and Joseph W. Beard
6. *Textbooks in School and Society*
   by Arthur Woodward, David L. Elliott, and
   Kathleen Carter Nagel
7. *Teacher Job Satisfaction*
   by Paula E. Lester
8. *Computers in Education*
   by Richard A. Diem
9. *Prevention Education*
   by William J. Derivan and Natalie Anne Silverstein
10. *Teacher Education Program Evaluation*
    by Jerry B. Ayers and Mary F. Berney
11. *Sex Differences and Learning: An Annotated Bibliography of Educational Research, 1979–1989*
    by Jean Dresden Grambs and John C. Carr

SEX DIFFERENCES AND LEARNING

An Annotated Bibliography of Educational Research, 1979–1989

Jean Dresden Grambs
John C. Carr

GARLAND PUBLISHING, INC. • NEW YORK & LONDON
1991

Library of Congress Cataloging-in-Publication Data

Grambs, Jean Dresden, 1919–
Sex differences and learning : an annotated bibliography of educational research, 1979–1989 / Jean Dresden Grambs, John C. Carr.
p. cm. — (Garland reference library of social science ; vol. 418) (Garland bibliographies in contemporary education ; vol. 11)
Includes index.
ISBN 0-8240-6641-3 (alk. paper)
1. Sex differences in education—United States—Bibliography.
2. Learning—Bibliography. I. Carr, John Charles, 1929– .
II. Title. III. Series: Garland reference library of social science ; v. 418. IV. Series: Garland bibliographies in contemporary education ; v. 11.
Z5815.U5G73 1991
[LC212.92]
016.37019'345—dc20 90-19600
CIP

Printed on acid-free, 250-year-life paper
Manufactured in the United States of America

In memory

of

Jean Dresden Grambs
1919-1989

She knew the differences
and celebrated them.

CONTENTS

ACKNOWLEDGMENTS

Deep appreciation is extended

. to Dr. Robert Hardy, Chair, Department of Human Development, University of Maryland College Park, who ensured secretarial support for Jean Grambs in the initial stages of this book,

.to Mary Jo Smith, who prepared a draft of the early research,

.to Kathleen Painter who served excellently as Dr. Grambs' research assistant,

.to Keith Maynard whose expertise as research assistant ensured completion of the manuscript,

.to Marie Ellen Larcada who was both patient and encouraging,

And most especially

.to Jane Nowosadko who saved the day by patiently making her way through draft after draft, and who prepared the camera-ready pages in splendid form and with splendid grace.

INTRODUCTION

The Context

Is the glass half full or half empty? Have we made strides in understanding and attending to the differences between how males and females learn? Or do the old conditions, based on ignorance, faulty assumptions, and outmoded social structures, persist?

Have we made strides? Yes, the glass is half full. Do the old conditions persist? Yes, the glass is half empty.

Sex Differences and Learning: An Annotated Bibliography of Educational Research, 1979-1989 testifies to our growing awareness of, and concern about, sex differences in the educational process. Its entries, selectively chosen from a larger field of research and commentary, enumerate something of that awareness and concern; coupled with reports and observations of changing attitudes, behavior, and practices in schools it suggests ways in which the glass may be said to be half full.

Increasingly, there is acknowledgment that the organization and operation of schools reinforce gender stereotypes. Language is under scrutiny, with attention drawn to how the official language of the educational establishment as well as the informal language of many administrators, teachers, and students, inhibits thinking and behavior when it is sexist in nature. Assessments of curriculum materials have led to changes ranging from a more balanced pictorial representation of males and females in occupations to increased content about contributions made by women in the arts, literature, science, and mathematics. Title IX has permitted freer access for both sexes in physical education, industrial arts, and home economics. In ways, not yet measured, it is clear that many more females than formerly are aware of opportunities to choose non-traditional occupations and lifestyles. Similarly, greater numbers of students are asserting themselves (if not always easily) in the face of sex discrimination.

At the same time, an examination of the studies annotated in the bibliography, coupled with reports and observations from schools, suggests ways in which the glass may be said to be half empty.

To a large degree schools continue to hold different standards for males and females, sending them ambiguous messages about academic expectations and social behavior. Males fail more often, have more serious encounters with authorities, and drop out more frequently than females. Females, too often, are not asked to, and do not, work to intellectual capacity. Simultaneously, large numbers of females are denied opportunities to develop their leadership capabilities. Success for males usually hinges on problem solving while success for females does not. Teachers respond differently to males and females in and out of the classroom, interacting more frequently with males, even if only in punitive ways. In the main, females continue to defer to the opinions and leadership of males. Mathematics, science, and computers (beyond word processing) continue to be viewed as male provinces. Students in teacher education programs have little or no direct exposure to issues of either sex differences or sex discrimination. School administrators demonstrate little inclination to confront sex differences issues except in politically "safe" ways.

While the evidence of research and practice draws us in both optimistic and pessimistic directions, surely that tension underscores the belief that sex differences and learning is a subject rich in opportunities for inquiry and discovery.

Sex Differences

While the subject of sex differences drew some attention before the 1960's, it did so only in secondary ways. Not until the publication of Macoby's ***The Development of Sex Differences***[1] in 1966 did it achieve validity as a central focus of research. Initially, scholarly concern appeared in the form of criticism of interpretations of sex-skewed research data and of assumptions about male and female biological, cognitive, and psychosocial capacities. Macoby and Jacklin's ***The Psychology of Sex Differences,***[2] published in 1974,

---

[1]Macoby, E.E. (1966). ***The Development of Sex Differences.*** Palo Alto: Stanford University Press.

[2]Macoby, E.E., & Jacklin, C.N. (1974). ***The Psychology of Sex Differences.*** Palo Alto: Stanford University Press.

galvanized the academic community with its wide-ranging and analytic discourse and helped ensure the subject of sex differences a respected place in social science research and beyond.

During the 1970's, important issues concerning sex differences research received close attention: philosophical points of view were honed; issues were clarified; many studies sought to identify male and female commonalities and distinctions. In the 1980's, researchers, building on the bulk of previous investigations, intensified the study of male and female development over the life span.

Sex Difference and Learning

Educational researchers, and others whose interests intersect with education, saw quickly the implications of sex differences research and learning. As studies in the encompassing subject have proliferated in the last 25 years, so have studies seeking to understand the role of gender in the educational process. The body of work, far more extensive than a volume of this kind can document, has

.challenged assumptions about the purposes and uses of educational research,

.contradicted earlier, less sophisticated, investigations,

.demonstrated the degree to which some educational practices shortchange students of both sexes,

.posed original and far-reaching questions important to the entire enterprise of schooling,

and

.served to "keep honest" the academic community in the pursuit of truth. (One of the efficacious results of sex differences research has been to ensure that all disciplines using human research subjects account for gender in order to prevent misreadings of data whose observed variance may be contributed by one sex.)

The endeavor to comprehend the role sex differences play in all aspects of our lives is a worthy one purely on academic grounds; such understanding is an important contribution to human knowledge. There is, however, an urgently important reason for understanding sex differences and learning, since those differences remind us of the much-vaunted goal of honoring the uniqueness of students. Failing to understand and to act upon how gender contributes to that uniqueness threatens both individual well-being and the public welfare.

Organization of the Bibliography

Sex Differences and Learning has been conceived as a tool to which professionals may turn for quick reference, for familiarity with a range of studies, and for assistance in identifying relevant research issues.

The book's organization is intended to be helpful to educational researchers, classroom teachers K-12, school administrators, curriculum developers, supervisory personnel, faculties and administrators of schools, colleges, and departments of education, and researchers outside education where it may have relevance.

The book took its form gradually. An initial broad survey of the literature on sex differences and learning from the last two decades yielded evidence of the degree to which this subject has won wide acceptance in a relatively short time. The range of material available was both great and diverse in nature, (1) appearing in journals, books, monographs, reports, and unpublished documents of various kinds, (2) extending in coverage from pre- to graduate school and inservice education, (3) presenting research and commentary, and (4) representing the work of professionals in many countries.

To prevent unwieldiness of bulk and to provide some measures of quality, it was necessary to establish limitations that would govern selection of entries for the bibliography. The first limitation was made in an effort to accomplish two ends: to comply with restrictions regarding length and to be as current as possible. Erring on the side of recency, then, entries were chosen only from the period 1979-1989.

Further efforts to shape the bibliography's content resulted in additional limitations. It was decided to choose entries only from

.research studies, except in a few instances where commentaries seemed especially appropriate,

.professional journals,

.studies using American subjects, except in instances involving cross-cultural study with Americans,

.research concerned with subjects in grades K-12, except (1) in instances where a direct link is made between subjects and some aspect of teacher behavior, and (2) where longitudinal studies extended outside, but included, grades K-12.

With these limitations in mind, another factor was used to screen selections: accessibility of the articles. Could one reasonably expect to find them in a good research library such as that found in most universities or in certain public and private circumstances?

When all the limitations were brought to bear, the remaining pool of material became immediately more manageable and lent itself more readily to topical divisions. As analysis continued, various categories--aligning themselves well with many central issues of schooling--emerged. As time passed, these categories were modified or replaced until the 23 categories of the bibliography solidified.

An alphabetic arrangement of categories was helpful in the editorial process and is intended to be helpful to readers as they examine the Contents and locate items within the bibliography.

Certainly, other editors would perceive other ways of selecting and arranging material for this kind of bibliography. The prevailing hope is that while other views may be equally valid, this one will prove valuable.

Readers will note that there are numerous entries in some categories--notably Language/Reading/Literature, Science, Mathematics, and Sex Roles/Socialization/Stereotyping--and relatively few in others--notably Help Seeking/Helping Behavior, Toys/Play/Games, School Attendance/Dropouts, and Mental Health/Mental Well-Being. While additional materials in some form exist for those categories, they do not fall within the established limitations for inclusion here. Generally speaking, however, the number of entries within categories reflects the quantity of material generated in the field at large.

Researchers, and those who support research, may take particular note of the paucity of sex difference studies in industrial arts and technological study, home economics, social studies, foreign languages, theatre, and dance.

Little or no research has been conducted with students in specialized school settings, such as magnet schools, mathematics and science high schools, vocational schools, schools-without-walls, and performing arts high schools. And few studies are concerned with students in rural and inner city schools.

Neglected is research on sex differences and learning as it pertains to students from itinerant, dysfunctional, and abusive families, to students who are bilingual, to those who are homosexual and lesbian, to those with handicapping conditions, and to those who are at risk for reasons of alcohol and drug abuse and homelessness. Asian and Hispanic students are seldom the subjects of study.

The topic of creativity is essentially ignored and so is the influence of popular culture. Religious affiliation and enrollment by private and parochial schools are additional variables for which little or no information is available.

The study of sex differences and learning is essentially bereft of research of a qualitative nature and of approaches in which quantitative and qualitative research are blended.

Using the Bibliography

To use ***Sex Differences and Learning*** successfully, it will be helpful, first of all, to examine the category titles. Numerous of them have multiple listings in order that appropriately related citations could be included.

The entries of the bibliography are numbered consecutively from the first category (Academic Achievement) through the last category (Toys/Play/Games). In many categories, cross references are made to entries annotated elsewhere. Cross references are marked by an asterisk.

Two indexes appear at the end of the book, one for authors and for subjects.

Sex Differences and Learning

Academic Achievement

1. Bordelon, K.W. (1985). Sexism in reading materials. **Reading Teacher, 38**(8), 792-97.

Reviews research dealing with two major questions: (1) Is sexism present in teaching materials? and (2) Are boys poorer readers than girls, and if so should teaching materials be geared to their interests?

2. Buys, N.J., & Winefield, A.H. (1982). Learned helplessness in high school students following experience of non-contingent rewards. **Journal of Research in Personality, 16**(1), 118-27.

Compares high school students differing in achievement motivation in a learned helplessness experiment. A strong helplessness effect was observed in both high-and low-achievement motivation groups. Results (1) show a strong learned helplessness effect unrelated to individual differences in achievement motivation, and (2) refute claims that helplessness depends on aversive outcomes. Sex differences are discussed.

3. Caskey, W.E., Jr., & Larson, G.L. (1983). Relationship between selected kindergarten predictors and first and fourth grade achievement test scores. **Perceptual and Motor Skills, 56**(3), 815-22.

Correlates kindergarten predictors, Otis-Lennon IQ, group and individual Bender scores, and teachers' ratings with first-grade Stanford

Achievement Test scores from local district and fourth-grade Ohio Survey Test scores from 102 of the same children. Sex differences are discussed.

4. Cole, T., & Sapp, G.L. (1988). Stress, locus of control, and achievement of high school seniors. **Psychological Reports, 63**(2), 355-359.

High school seniors in the top and bottom achievement quartiles responded to the Nowicki-Strickland Locus of Control Scale and Bowden's Tension-Stress (TS) Test. Results indicate that internally oriented students showed lower TS than externally oriented ones. Girls scored higher than boys on life changes associated with TS.

5. Dietz, C., & Wilson, B.J. (1985). Beginning school age and academic achievement. **Psychology in the Schools, 22**(1), 93-94.

Studies effects of beginning school age and gender on later school achievement and retention in grade. No significant differences among the three age groups were found at kindergarten, second, or fourth grade. Differences in achievement between boys and girls are noted.

6. DiPasquale, G.W., et al. (1980). The birthdate effect. **Journal of Learning Disabilities, 13**(5), 234-38.

Findings of this study support theory that children born late in the year are significantly more likely to be referred for academic problems in the primary grades than are children born early in the year. Sex differences are discussed.

7. Englehard, G., Jr., & Monsaas, J.A. (1989). Academic performance, gender, and the cooperative attitudes of third, fifth, and seventh graders. **Journal of Research and Development in Education, 22**(2), 13-17.

Reports results of an investigation of the links between academic performance, gender, and the cooperative attitudes of elementary students. Data show successful students reported less cooperative attitudes than unsuccessful students, and while third grade girls reported higher cooperative attitudes than boys, no gender differences were found in the fifth and seventh grades.

8. Evans, E.D., & Engelberg, R.A. (1988). Student perceptions of school grading. **Journal of Research and Development in Education, 21**(2), 45-54.

Reports results of a questionnaire administered to students, grades four through eleven, regarding their viewpoints on grades. Three dimensions were examined: (1) attitudes about being graded; (2) comprehension of grading systems; and (3) causal perceptions and attributions about why students get good grades. Sex differences are discussed.

9. Finn, J.D. (1980). Sex differences in educational outcomes: a cross-national study. **Sex Roles: A Journal of Research, 6**(1), 9-26.

Cross-national data on 14-year-old children in England, Sweden and the United States are analyzed for sex differences in achievement and attitudes in science and reading. School characteristics associated with large sex discrepancies are identified.

10. Finn, J.D., et al. (1979). Sex differences in educational attainment: a cross-national perspective. **Harvard Educational Review, 49**(4), 477-503.

A review of cross-national studies of educational attainment reveals that, regardless of type of educational system or extent of opportunity, females are universally disadvantaged educationally.

11. Gullo, D.F., et al. (1986). A comparative study of "all-day," "alternate-day" and "half-day" kindergarten schedules: effects on achievement and classroom social behaviors. **Journal of Research in Childhood Education, 1**(2), 87-94.

Compares the relative effects of three different kindergarten schedules (all-day, half-day, alternating day) on children's end-of-the-year achievement and prosocial classroom behaviors. All-day kindergarten children scored higher on achievement than the other groups. Alternating day kindergarten children were lower on negative social behavior factors. Sex differences are discussed.

12. Hahn, C.L. (1982). Are there gender differences in high school economics in the eighties? **Journal of Economic Education, 13**(2), 57-65.

Compares achievement of male and female high school students in a required economics course. Course grades and standardized test scores for 1412 students were examined for possible gender-related causes of differences in achievement levels. Results show no significant differences between male and female student performance.

13. Haynes, N.M., & Comer, J.P., & Hamilton-Lee, M. (1988). Gender and achievement status differences on learning factors among black high school students. **Journal of Educational Research, 81**(4), 233-237.

Reports results of administering the Learning and Study Strategy Inventory to black female and male urban 10th graders divided into high-, average-, and low-achieving groups on basis of grade averages. Regression analyses suggest a different set of study strategies was important for males and females; however, motivation was the strongest predictor of grade average among both sexes.

14. Kamalanabhan, T.J. (1988). Efficacy of a behavioral program for personality change and improvement in academic performance of school students. **Journal of Psychological Research, 32**(1-2), 93-101.

Investigates the efficacy of a behavioral program consisting of relaxation, assertiveness, and study skills training for personality change and improvement in the academic performance of 12-15 year-olds. Results show that the training program proved effective in modifying the students' personality and improving their academic performance.

15. Keith, T.Z. (1988). Using path analysis to test the importance of manipulable influences on school learning. **School Psychology Review, 17**(4), 637-643.

Reports development of a general path model based on variables common to theories of school learning. Various influences on the achievement of nearly 26,000 high school students are reported. Direct, indirect, and total effects of each variable of interest were calculated and interpreted. Sex differences are discussed.

* Kinard, E.M., & Reinherz, H. (1987). School aptitude and achievement in children of adolescent mothers. **Journal of Youth and Adolescence.** (Cited as entry 234.)

16. Kneedler, P.E. (1988). Differences between boys and girls on California's new statewide assessments in history--social science. **Social Studies Review, 27**(3), 96-124.

Describes and illustrates performance differences observed between boys and girls on California's history--social science assessments. Provides recommendations for reducing differences.

17. Kurder, L.A., & Sinclair, R.J. (1988). Relation of eighth graders' family structure, gender, and family environment with academic performance and school behavior. **Journal of Educational Psychology, 80**(1), 90-94.

Reports assessment of family structure, gender, and family environment and relationship to academic performance and school behavior for middle class eighth grade students. Generally, students in two-parent nuclear families had better academic performance and less problematic school behavior than did students in either mother-custody or stepfather families. Boys had more detentions than did girls.

18. Langer, P., et al. (1984). Age of admission and trends in

achievement: a comparison of blacks and caucasians. **Educational Research Journal, 21**(1), 61-78.

Investigates the changing achievement relationships among black and white students based on ages at entry into first grade. Data indicates that, for both groups, significantly higher achievement of the oldest students at age 9 disappeared by age 17. Sex differences are discussed.

19. Lao, R.C. (1980). Differential factors affecting male and female academic performance in high school. **Journal of Psychology, 114**(2), 119-27.

Reports findings that highly achievement-motivated, internal, independent female students got the highest grades. Indicates that some factors influencing achievement operate differently for males than for females.

20. Lewis, H.P., & Livson, N. (1980). Cognitive development, personality and drawing: their interrelationships in a replicated longitudinal study. **Studies in Art Education, 22**(1), 8-11.

Reports results of a study of 72 children for whom the following data were available: IQ score on a conventional test (WISC or Stanford-Binet); Goodenough-Harris drawing test IQ score; and behavior description by the test administrator. Assesses personality traits of children performing better on either graphic or conventional IQ test. Sex differences are discussed.

21. Licht, B.G., Stader, S.R., & Swenson, C.C. (1989). Children's achievement-related beliefs: effects of academic area, sex and achievement level. **Journal of Educational Research, 82**(5), 253-260.

Examines fifth graders' academic self-concepts, causal attributions, and perceptions of teacher feedback by function of academic area, achievement level, and sex. Girls rated themselves as less smart than boys in social studies and science, but not in math or reading. Sex differences were found in causal attributions.

22. Macy, D.J., et al. (1979). An empirical study of the Myklebust Learning Quotient. **Journal of Learning Disabilities, 12**(2), 93-96.

Reports computing of learning quotients for second, fourth, sixth, and eighth graders. Findings indicate that the learning quotients were not statistically stable across tests, grade level, gender, or ethnicity.

23. Manahan, J. (1984). Student attitude and gender in principles of economics. **Journal of Business Education, 59**(7), 257-61.

Examines relationships among students' achievement or knowledge, students' gender, and students' attitude toward economics as a discipline.

24. Marsh, H.W. (1986). Self-serving effect (Bias?) in academic attributions: its relation to academic achievement and self-concept. **Journal of Educational Psychology, 78**(3), 190-200.

Examines self-serving effect (SSE), the tendency to accept responsibility for one's own successes but not failures, in three studies with adolescents: (1) academic self-concepts; (2) academic self-concepts inferred by significant others; and (3) academic achievement. Sex differences are discussed.

25. Miller, L.B., & Bizzell, R.P. (1983). Long-term effects of four preschool programs: sixth, seventh, and eighth grades. **Child Development, 54**(3), 727-41.

Investigates academic and intellectual performance of disadvantaged children who had experienced one of four types of prekindergarten program or no prekindergarten at all. IQ measures show no significant change among preschool program groups, but differential effects in the three grades, related to both preschool program and sex, are noted in reading and math.

26. Nowak, T. (1981). "Fear of success": a classroom experiment. **History and Social Science Teacher, 16**(3), 184-86.

Reports results of a classroom experiment in which students completed a creative writing assignment based on sex differences in achievement motivation and performance. Findings show that females demonstrated motives to avoid success while males seemed not to want to accept the idea of female achievement.

27. Osterlind, S.J. (1980). Preschool impact on children: its sustaining effects into kindergarten. **Educational Research Quarterly, 5**(4), 21-30.

Reports results of a study comparing kindergarten pupils who had previously attended preschool with those who had not. Reading (or reading readiness) and mathematics achievement, academic potential, social and emotional maturity, conformity to successful pupil behaviors, and adjustment to academic and social setting in the classroom were examined. Sex differences are discussed.

* Pittman, R.B. (1979). Situational referents of an academic setting and locus of control. **Journal of Experimental Education.** (Cited as entry 573.)

28. Schneider, F.W., & Coutts, L.M. (1985). Person orientation of male and female high school students: to the educational disadvantage of males? **Sex Roles: A Journal of Research, 13**(1-2), 47-63.

Investigates differences in person orientation of male and female high school students that may have significant influences on their achievement strivings. Boys are particularly susceptible to anti-intellectual influences from peers. Interference of affiliative concerns with achievement behavior may not be relevant in understanding males' academic under-achievement.

* Sexton, L.C., & Treloar, J.H. (1979). Auditory and visual perception, sex, and academic aptitude as predictors of achievement for first-grade children. **Measurement and Evaluation in Guidance.** (Cited as entry 523.)

29. Sexton, L.C., & Treloar, J.H. (1982). Cognitive and perceptual measures as predictors of fourth-grade achievement. **Psychology in the Schools, 19**(1), 122-28.

Uses a multi-variate approach and longitudinal design to examine the relationship of early perceptual and cognitive development in first grade to school achievement in fourth grade. Results indicate that variables used to predict achievement differed between the sexes, and that sex as a predictor variable depended upon area of achievement.

30. Smith, T.L. (1988). Self concept and teacher expectation of academic achievement in elementary school children. **Journal of Instructional Psychology, 15**(2), 78-83.

Investigates relationship of self-concept of 3rd-6th graders to teacher expectation of academic achievement. A 3-way factorial (sex by race by grade level) yielded a significant self-concept difference according to sex, with girls having higher self-concept scores than boys.

* Steelman, L.C., & Powell, B. (1985). The social and academic consequences of birth order: real, artificial, or both? **Journal of Marriage and the Family.** (Cited as entry 752.)

31. Stipek, D.J., & Hoffman, J.M. (1980). Children's achievement-related expectancies as a function of academic performance histories and sex. **Journal of Educational Psychology, 72**(6), 861-65.

High-, average-, and low-achieving boys and girls in the first and third grades are compared on their expectations for success prior to an anagrams task, their subsequent perceptions of the cause of failure on the task, and their expectations for future success.

32. Stockard, J., et al. (1985). Academic merit, status variables, and student grades. **Journal of Research and Development in Education, 18**(2), 12-20.

Studies the effect of ability, social class, gender, and achievement on students' grades by examining standardized test results in mathematics and English courses.

33. Swartz, J.P., & Walker, D.K. (1984). The relationship between teacher ratings of kindergarten classroom skills and second grade achievement scores: an analysis of gender differences. **Journal of School Psychology, 22**(2), 209-17.

Uses the Kindergarten Performance Profile to analyze the relationship of classroom skills in the fall and spring of kindergarten to second grade achievement. Results indicate kindergarten work skills were related significantly to achievement for both boys and girls.

34. Tann, S. (1979). A study of group work. **Forum for the Discussion of New Trends in Education, 21**(3), 91-95.

Records and analyzes 96 student discussion groups to identify successful dialogue strategies, to highlight difficulties deriving from group characteristics, to examine how students behave, to determine what they gain, and to identify which students benefit most. Sex differences are discussed.

35. Webb, N.W. (1985). Cognitive requirements of learning computer programming in group and individual settings. **AEDS Journal, 18**(3), 183-94.

Compares achievement of students learning computer programming in pairs and individually and examines relationships between cognitive abilities, style, and demographics. Mathematics and verbal ability best predicted outcomes for students working individually, while nonverbal reasoning, spatial ability, and age best predicted learning in groups. Sex differences are discussed.

36. Worthington, G.B., III, & Bening, M.E. (1988). Use of the Kaufman Assessment Battery for Children in predicting achievement among students referred for special education services. **Journal of Learning Disabilities, 21**(6), 370-74.

Reports the Kaufman Assessment Battery for Children (K-ABC) valid in predicting reading, mathematics, and written expression for black, Hispanic, and white male students referred for special education services. Scores are not valid predictors, however, of written language achievement for referred females.

37. Zwick, R., & Ercikan, K. (1989). Analysis of differential item functioning in the NAEP history assessment. **Journal of Educational Measurement, 26**(1), 55-66.

Reports results of an analysis using the Mantel-Haenszel approach for investigating differential item functioning (DIF) applied to United States history items within 1986 National Assessment of Educational Progress administered to 7,812 11th graders. DIF analyses were based on responses of 7,743 11th graders. Results concerning sex and racial differences and ethnicity are provided.

Career and Occupational Interests and Goals

38. Adams, G.R., & Hicken, M. (1984). Historical-cultural change in the expression of vocational preference and expectation by preschool and elementary school age children. **Family Relations, 33**(2), 301-07.

Replicates Looft's 1971 study on vocational preference and expectation using preschool and primary students. Results show modest changes in occupational preferences, still mediated by sex role assumptions. Results show girls' expectations of obtaining preferred occupations as very low.

39. Barnhart, R.S. (1983). Children's sex-typed views of traditional occupational roles. **School Counselor, 31**(2), 167-70.

Examines children's views of traditional occupations in a study of elementary school students who viewed photographs of 18 occupations. Students chose traditional male or female roles in most instances.

40. Chester, N.L. (1983). Sex differentiation in two high school environments: implications for career development among black adolescent females. **Journal of Social Issues, 39**(3), 29-40.

Compares black males and females on career-related variables. Students were enrolled in a predominantly white liberal arts school and also in an integrated vocational high school. Results show that females attending the former had lower aspirations and self-esteem.

41. Copa, G.H., & Forsberg, G.D. (1981). Employment and further education effects of secondary vocational education in Minnesota. **Journal of Vocational Education Research, 6**(3), 1-18.

Investigates "reasonable" expectations for post high school employment and further education of secondary school vocation students. Sex differences are discussed.

42. Culver, S.M., & Burge, P.L. (1985). Expected occupational prestige of students in vocational programs non-traditional for their sex. **Journal of Studies in Technical Careers, 7**(4), 231-40.

Examines differences in occupational aspirations of students grouped by sex and by predominance of sex enrolled in vocational programs. Females in male-predominant, female-predominant, and sex equal programs had higher aspirations than males in each of these groups.

43. Danziger, N. (1983). Sex-related differences in the aspirations of high school students. **Sex Roles: A Journal of Research, 9**(6), 683-95.

Reports results of a study showing male high school students' educational and career aspirations strongly influenced by their academic ability and achievement and females' aspirations influenced mainly by parental attitudes and their socioeconomic background.

44. Davies, M., & Kandel, D.B. (1981). Parental and peer influences on adolescents' educational plans: some further evidence. **American Journal of Sociology, 87**(2), 363-87.

Reports results of a study of adolescent perceptions showing parents have more influence on their children's educational aspirations than do their children's best friends. Parental influence appears to grow stronger over time. Best friends influence girls' aspirations more than boys.

45. Donovan, E.P., et al. (1985). A new science and engineering career interest survey for middle school students. **Journal of Research in Science Teaching, 22**(1), 19-30.

Describes the development and validation of a 56-item science and engineering career interest survey for seventh through ninth grade students. The survey includes questions on occupational activities, selection of occupations, and an internal verification scale. Results indicate significant differences in career interest for boys and girls.

46. Dorn, F.J., & Welch, N. (1985). Assessing career mythology: a profile of high school students. **School Counselor, 33**(2), 136-42.

Examines extent to which career mythology exists in a sample high school population using the Survey of Career Attitudes. Results indicate that the sample met the established criterion for the career myths of Quitters Never Win, Sex Roles, The Perfect Job, and My Child the Doctor. Criteria for nine other myths were not met. Sex differences are discussed.

47. Dunne, F., et al. (1981). Sex differences in the educational and occupational aspirations of rural youth. **Journal of Vocational Behavior, 18**(1), 56-66.

Reports results of a study of rural girls, answering questions concerning educational and occupational aspirations. Findings show significantly higher educational aspiration, the same or higher occupational aspiration, and equal ranges of job choice, relative to boys.

48. Durkin, K., & Hutchins, G. (1984). Challenging traditional sex role stereotypes in careers education broadcasts: the reactions of young secondary school pupils. **Journal of Educational Television, 10**(1), 25-33.

Secondary school pupils' reactions to viewing careers education materials showing people in occupations traditionally associated with the opposite sex were no less stereotyped in career beliefs than those viewing counter-stereotyped materials.

49. Ekstrom, R.B., et al. (1987). The effects of youth employment program participation on later employment. **Evaluation Review, 11**(1), 84-101.

A three-year follow-up of a national sample of youth employment training program participants and nonparticipants of comparable background showed that participants obtained more months of employment and had greater job satisfaction. Program effectiveness was greater for minority than non-minority youth and greater for females than male.

50. Fouad, N.A. (1988). The construct of career maturity in the United States and Israel. **Journal of Vocational Behavior, 32**(1), 49-59.

Investigates construct of career maturity in United States and Israel by assessing attitudes about career decision making among U.S. and Israeli ninth and twelfth grade students on the Career Maturity Inventory (CMI). Findings show (1) differences across cultures in career maturity and (2) sex differences on some individual subscales of the CMI.

51. Hageman, M.B., & Gladding, S.T. (1983). The art of career exploration: occupational sex-role stereotyping among elementary school children. **Elementary School Guidance and Counseling, 17**(4), 280-87.

Studies occupational sex-role stereotyping among elementary school children. In addition to a questionnaire, students drew themselves in the occupation they would most likely choose. Most girls chose "female" occupations.

52. Herzog, A.R. (1982). High school seniors' occupational plans and values: trends in sex differences 1976 through 1980. **Sociology of Education, 55**(1), 1-13.

Examines occupational plans and values of high school seniors for evidence of declining sex differences between 1976-1980. Questionnaire data collected from 3,000 students indicates marked sex differences in the kinds of work boys and girls planned to do at age 30 and the work settings and characteristics they desired.

53. Hoffman, E.P. (1987). Determinants of youths' educational and occupational goals: sex and race differences. **Economics of Education Review, 6**(1), 41-48.

Using national longitudinal survey data for 1966-68 and 1979, this study explores possible differences between the educational and occupational goals of black and white male and female youths. Occupational and educational goals are seen as related, and while sex and race differences exist, they have changed over time.

54. Holcomb, C.A. (1981). My daughter wants to be a nurse: occupational stereotyping in health textbooks. **Journal of School Health, 51**(5), 336-40.

An evaluation of the illustrations in elementary and secondary education textbooks. Conclusions show: (1) males dominate occupations illustrated in contemporary health textbooks, and (2) females generally are portrayed as assistants (nurses, technicians, dental hygienists).

55. Horne, M.D., & Kaufman, R. (1979). Occupational attitudes: a comparison of monolingual and bilingual student groups. **The Journal for the National Association for Bilingual Education, 3**(3), 61-69.

Discusses possibly significant effect of social acceptance and negligible effects of culture and sex on attitudes of bilingual and monolingual fourth grade students towards occupational groups. Discusses children's early awareness of society's attitudes towards occupations and probable existence of a reasonably stable hierarchy of occupational preference.

* Hughes, C.M., et al. (1985). Sex role attitudes and career

choices: the role of children's self-esteem. **Elementary School Guidance and Counseling.** (Cited as entry 659.)

* Jacobowitz, T. (1983). Relationship of sex, achievement, and science self-concept to the science career preferences of black students. **Journal of Research in Science Teaching.** (Cited as entry 599.)

56. Johnson, R.G. (1985). Microcomputer-assisted career exploration. **Vocational Guidance Quarterly, 33**(4), 296-304.

High school students participated in traditional and computer-assisted career exploration. Results indicate no differences in career exploratory behaviors or options selected. Students did, however, favor the computer-assisted treatment. No sex differences were found.

* Kahle, J.B., et al. (1985). An assessment of the impact of science experiences on the career choices of male and female biology students. **Journal of Research in Science Teaching.** (Cited as entry 603.)

57. Kammer, P.P. (1985). Career and life-style expectations of rural eighth-grade students. **School Counselor, 33**(1), 18-25.

Examines relationship between sex and career and life-style expectations of 128 students. Results indicate no sex differences in curricular or post-secondary plans. Equal proportions of males and females indicated professional career aspirations; however, they differed in their choices along traditional lines. Males expected to achieve their career goals more than females.

58. Koppel, R., & DelRoccili, J. (1982). Urban education and student prospects: policy implications. **Urban Education, 16**(4), 49-63.

Examines the determinants of occupational and educational aspirations and expectations of adolescents. Dependent variables considered in the study included parents' occupational status and education, and students' grade level, sex, ethnicity, reading level, and knowledge of the work world.

59. Krummel, M., & Cole, R.L. (1987). Perceptions of vocational and agriculture competencies and sex equity in Oregon. **Journal of the American Association of Teacher Educators in Agriculture, 28**(1), 50-55.

A survey of male and female secondary students and teachers in vocational agriculture attempting to determine if sex equity had been perceptually established on a competency-level attainment basis within six taxonomy areas. Subjects perceived no gender differences in competency-level attainment in most taxonomies.

60. Lee, C.C. (1984). An investigation of the psychological variables in the occupational aspirations and expectations of rural black and white adolescents: implications for vocational education. **Journal of Research and Development in Education, 17**(3), 28-34.

Rural 10th-grade students revealed that both race and sex differences affected their occupational aspirations. Parental influence, socioeconomic status, and self-concept were also influential. Implications for future rural vocational education are discussed.

61. MacKay, W.R., & Miller, C.A. (1982). Relations of socioeconomic status and sex variables to the complexity of worker functions in the occupational choices of elementary school children. **Journal of Vocational Behavior, 20**(1), 31-39.

Children's occupational choices were scored for complexity using the code numbers of the Occupational Titles. Findings indicated a positive relationship between socioeconomic status and complexity of data manipulation in occupational choices and greater complexity of interaction with things in the occupational choices of boys.

* Matheny, A.P., et al. (1980). Cognitive aspects of interests, responsibilities and vocational goals in adolescence.

Adolescence. (Cited as entry 102.)

62. Neely, M.A. (1980). Career maturity inventory interpretations for grade 9 boys and girls. **Vocational Guidance Quarterly, 29**(2), 113-23.

Boys and girls in grade 9 are expected to master the same developmental tasks, yet a review of literature suggests that by grade 9 boys experience pre-career anxiety, while girls experience premature closure of opportunities. Findings call for sex-based norms on the Career Maturity Inventory.

63. Neely, M.A., & Johnson, C.W. (1981). The relationship of performance on six scales of the Career Development Inventory to sex, father's education, and father's occupation. **Educational and Psychological Measurement, 41**(3), 917-21.

An examination of the performance of 10th grade boys and girls on six career development inventory subscales through use of a three-way multi-variate analysis of variance (MANOVA) on sex, father's education, and father's occupation.

64. Price-Curtis, W., & Jarvis, C.H. (1982). An examination of the variables related to minority youth employment. **Journal of Employment Counseling, 19**(2), 67-75.

Examines post-program experiences of minority youth in the National Urban League Youth Career Development Project. Results confirm difficulties minority female teenagers have obtaining jobs. Findings show parents' employment status had little effect and that unemployed youth tended to rely on informal job search techniques.

65. Super, D.E., & Nevill, D.D. (1984). Work role salience as a determinant of career maturity in high school students. **Journal of Vocational Behavior, 25**(1), 30-44.

A test of eight hypotheses concerning relationships between socioeconomic status, sex, work importance, and career maturity with high school students. Results indicated work salience (but not socioeconomic status) directly related to career maturity.

66. Tinsley, H.E., et al. (1984). The effects of values clarification exercises on the value structure of junior high school students. **Vocational Guidance Quarterly, 32**(3), 160-67.

Examines effectiveness of a two week values clarification program (career decision making, occupational information, leisure activities, and affective discussion) for junior high school students. Results indicate a greater degree of confusion, no sex differences, and differential effects for 7th and 8th graders.

67. Tremaine, L.S., & Schau, C.G. (1979). Sex-Role aspects in the development of children's vocational knowledge. **Journal of Vocational Behavior, 14**(3), 317-28.

Examines several dimensions of job choices in children of four age groups. Findings show older children more selective in personal job choice, especially regarding jobs attributed to the opposite sex.

68. Vockell, E.L., & Lobonc, S. (1981). Sex-role stereotyping by high school females in science. **Journal of Research in Science Teaching, 18**(3), 209-19.

Examines two questions: (1) Do high school students perceive the physical sciences as more masculine career fields than the biological sciences?; (2) What is the influence of coeducation on these sex-stereotyped positions?

69. Westbrook, B.W., et al. (1988). Career maturity in grade 9: can students who make appropriate career choices for others also make appropriate career choices for themselves? **Measurement and Evaluation in Counseling and Development, 21**(2), 64-71.

Reports results of administering the Career Maturity Inventory and the Differential Aptitude Test (Form V) to black and white ninth graders. No relationship between black students' ability to make appropriate career choices for themselves and their ability to make career choices for others is shown. A weak but significant relationship between these abilities was found for white students. Sex differences are discussed.

70. Wilson, J., & Daniel, R. (1981). The effects of a career-options workshop on social and vocational stereotypes. **Vocational Guidance Quarterly, 29**(4), 341-49.

Investigates the effects of a one-week career-options workshop on the stereotypical social and vocational attitudes of middle school students. Results show a brief workshop program could be effective in influencing traditional sex role attitudes.

71. Wilson, S. (1982). A new decade: the gifted and career choice. **Vocational Guidance Quarterly, 31**(1), 53-59.

Reports results of attempts to determine the careers gifted females and males plan, reasons for their choices, and aspects they consider most important in a job. Considers whether gifted females enter traditionally male fields in numbers comparable to gifted males.

Cognitive Styles | Cognitive Structures

72. Allen, D.A. & Hennessey, S., Jr. (1980). Children's location of a point in space: effects of dimensionality and salience of frame of reference. **Journal of Genetic Psychology, 136**(1), 151-52.

Examines the effects of dimensionality and salience of frame of reference on children's location of a point in space. Sex differences are discussed.

73. Anooshian, L.J., & Young, D. (1981). Developmental changes in cognitive maps of a familiar neighborhood. **Child Development, 52**(1), 341-48.

Children's performances in pointing a telescope at landmarks surrounding their own neighborhood were assessed for children in three age groups. Findings show sex differences both in point consistency and in accuracy of pointings from imagined reference sites.

74. Ayers, J.B., et al. (1979). Geometric embedded figure identification and construction by lower grade children. **School Science and Mathematics, 79**(8), 677-89.

Investigates differences in boys and girls in three grade levels of the identification and construction of embedded and overlapping figures and the effect of instruction on identification. Only significant differences shown are across grade levels in construction. Sex differences are discussed.

75. Bem, S.L. (1981). Gender schema theory: a cognitive account of sex typing. **Psychological Review, 88**(4), 354-64.

Gender schema theory proposes that sex typing derives from gender-based schematic processing, particularly from the self-concept itself being assimilated to the gender schema. In two studies sex-typed individuals showed greater readiness to process information (including information about the self) according to gender schema.

76. Benbow, C.P., & Stanley, J.C. (1980). Intellectually talented students: family profiles. **Gifted Child Quarterly, 24**(3), 119-22.

Describes family profiles compiled from analysis of questionnaires completed by Study of Mathematically Precocious Youth Talent Search participants (mostly seventh graders). Sex differences are discussed.

77. Benbow, C.P., et al. (1983). Structure of intelligence in intellectually precocious children and in their parents. **Intelligence, 7**(2), 129-52.

Students of high intellectual ability and their parents were tested on a battery of cognitive tests. Among children, age related to verbal but not spatial or mechanical abilities. Sex differences are discussed.

78. Berlin, D.F., & Languis, M.L. (1981). Hemispheric correlates of the rod-and-frame test. **Perceptual and Motor Skills, 52**(1), 35-41.

Reports results of administering the WISC Block Design and verbal and nonverbal versions of the Rod-and-Frame Test (RFT), measuring field dependence/independence, to right-handed sixth graders. Findings seem to reflect a right hemisphere processing for the nonverbal RFT and a possible sex bias against girls in its traditional verbal administration.

* Block, J.H. (1981). The difference between boys and girls: how

gender roles are shaped. **Principal.** (Cited as entry 642.)

79. Carvajal, H., et al. (1988). Relationships between scores on Stanford-Binet IV and Wechsler Preschool and Primary Scale of Intelligence. **Psychology in the Schools, 25**(2), 129-31.

Reports results of administering the 1986 Stanford-Binet Intelligence Scale (Fourth Edition) and the Wechsler Preschool and Primary Scale of Intelligence to a kindergarten class. Sex differences are discussed.

80. Cox, D.E., et al. (1988). Learning style variations among vocational agriculture students. **Journal of the American Association of Teacher Educators in Agriculture, 29**(1), 11-19, 44.

Reports results of administering The Secondary Learning Styles Inventory to vocational agriculture high school students in Arizona. Findings suggest that learning style characteristics vary by grade level, courses completed, and gender.

81. de Hernandez, L., et al. (1984). Relationships among gender, age, and intellectual development. **Journal of Research in Science Teaching, 21**(4), 365-75.

Reports results of a study in which males demonstrated a higher level of intellectual development than females and males matured intellectually earlier than females. Additionally, factors other than age and sex appeared to be related to development of formal operational reasoning.

82. De Lisi, R., & Smith, J.K. (1979). The reliability of Oltman's Rod-and-Frame Test with grade-school children. **Applied Psychological Measurement, 3**(3), 413-14.

Assesses the reliability of Oltman's Portable Rod and Frame Test (PRFT) with first-, third-, and fifth-grade children. Sex differences are discussed.

83. DeLuca, F.P. (1981). Application of cluster analysis to the study of Piagetian stages of intellectual development. **Journal of Research in Science Teaching, 18**(1), 51-59.

Reports results of a study (1) reexamining Piagetian stages of males and females ages nine to eighteen, using cluster analysis, (2) seeking information concerning occurrence of stages and influence of different tasks and gender on cluster patterns. Findings indicate deviation from Piagetian stages was influenced by gender and type of task.

84. Doyle, J.J. (1980). The order of attainment of eight projective groupings: an analysis of Piaget's Spatial Model. **Journal of Research in Science Teaching, 17**(1), 55-58.

Examines the attainment of projective spatial concepts of third-, sixth-, and ninth-grade students. Eight Piagetian-type tasks were developed to provide evidence for Piaget's model of groupings of mental structures dealing with time and space. Task performance among grade levels and gender are examined.

85. Eno, L., & Woehlke, P. (1980). Diagnostic differences between educationally handicapped and learning disabled students. **Psychology in the Schools, 17**(4), 469-73.

Reports results of a study in which unexpected sex differences are reported.

86. Farmer, W.A., et al. (1982). A validity study of two paper-pencil tests of concrete and formal operations. **Journal of Research in Science Teaching, 19**(6), 475-85.

Determines the degree to which classification of students as formal or concrete (based on three Inhelder tasks administered by clinical interview method) was mirrored by Longeot and Karplus-Lawson-Renner (KLR) classifications. Results indicate that Longeot and KLR differentiate between concrete/formal operations and are discussed from perspective of practitioner and researcher. Sex differences are discussed.

87. Hall, E.G. (1980). Sex differences in IQ development for intellectually gifted students. **Roeper Review, 2**(3), 25-28.

Reports results of a study showing that more girls had fathers with doctoral degrees, that girls' arithmetic and spatial abilities were not significantly different from boys', that girls increased or decreased in IQ more than boys in high school, and that boys' IQs and grade point averages were significantly correlated but girls' were not.

* Harty, H., et al. (1987). Gender influences on concept structure interrelatedness competence. **Science Education.** (Cited as entry 594.)

88. Herman, J.F., et al. (1982). Effects of motor activity on children's intentional and incidental memory for spatial locations. **Child Development, 53**(1), 239-44.

Examines (1) the effect of increased motor involvement with an environment on children's memory for spatial locations, and (2) the effect of different degrees of motor involvement under intentional and incidental memory conditions. Thirty boys and 30 girls at each of kindergarten and third-grade levels were individually tested in a large-scale, simulated model town. Sex differences are discussed.

89. Hurtig, A.L. (1985). Cognitive mediators of ego functioning in adolescence. **Journal of Youth and Adolescence, 14**(5), 435-50.

Examines relationships between ego functioning in adolescence and two domains of operational thinking (social interpersonal reasoning and physical-mathematical reasoning) in high school seniors. Results indicate significant differences between males and females in patterns of correlations and in patterns of relationships in a causal analysis.

90. Karnes, F.A., & Brown, K.E. (1980). Sex differences in the WISC-R scores of gifted students. **Psychology in the Schools, 17**(1), 361-63.

Reports results showing majority of differences in this study favor males. Abilities measured by the coding subtest are present to a greater extent in females, regardless of the level of intelligence. Gifted boys are reported manifesting a higher level of verbal intelligence than gifted girls.

91. Karnes, F.A., & Brown, K.E. (1980). Factor analysis of the WISC-R for the gifted. **Journal of Educational Psychology, 72**(2), 197-99.

Reports results of administering the Wechsler Intelligence Scale for Children--Revised to 946 intellectually gifted students, age 6 to 16. Factor structure was remarkably similar to that reported for previously studied groups, thus supporting test's validity. Sex differences are discussed.

92. Kaufman, N.L. (1980). Differential validity of reversal errors as predictors of first-grade reading achievement for blacks and whites. **Psychology in the Schools, 17**(4), 460-65.

Reports results of a study in which white children scored significantly higher than black children on the reversals test, although predictive validity coefficients were substantial for both races. Sex differences tended to be minor and of little consequence.

* Kishta, M.A. (1979). Proportional and combinatorial reasoning in two cultures. **Journal of Research in Science Teaching.** (Cited as entry 161.)

93. Klein, J.D., et al. (1987). The effect of age of viewer and gender of the narrator on children's visual attention and recall of story ideas. **Educational Communication and Technology Journal, 35**(4), 231-38.

Reports results of a study investigating interaction between the age of viewer and the gender of narrator of a film. Sex differences are discussed.

94. Koblinsky, S.A., & Cruse, D.F. (1981). The role of frameworks in children's retention of sex-related story content.

Journal of Experimental Child Psychology, 31(2), 321-31.

Examines the role of frameworks in children's memory for sex-related story information. Children displayed superior memory for sex-stereotypic content regardless of whether information was congruent or incongruent with societal sex role stereotypes. Results confirm that frameworks affect encoding more than recall.

95. Krebs, E. (1983). A study of the relationship of moral development and social interest to vocational maturity of adolescents. **Contemporary Education, 54**(4), 299-305.

Investigates the relationships among vocational, moral, and social development in ninth- and twelfth-grade students and the classification of psychological and psychosocial aspects of vocational maturity. Effects of age differences and sex differences are discussed.

96. Kreitler, S., et al. (1983). The effects of memory and abstractive integration on children's probability learning. **Child Development, 54**(6), 1487-96.

Examines the relation between children's (1) probability learning performance and a measure of their memory for items presented in a sequence and (2) probability learning and performance on a test of abstractive integration. Sex differences are discussed.

97. Lazarowitz, R. (1981). Correlations of junior high school students' age, gender, and intelligence with ability in construct classification in biology. **Journal of Research in Science Teaching, 18**(1), 15-22.

Reports results of a study to (1) develop an instrument requiring several classification activities, (2) investigate the correlation between classification ability and intelligence scores of junior high school students, and (3) determine if classification ability differs with age and gender.

98. Lee, K.S. (1982). Fourth graders' heuristic problem-solving

behavior. **Journal for Research in Mathematics Education, 13**(2), 110-23.

Reports results of a study in which specific heuristics were adopted from Polya. Students represented two substages of Piaget's concrete operational stage. Five hypotheses were generated, based on observed results and the study's theoretical rationale. Sex differences are discussed.

99. Levin, I., et al. (1984). The role of memory and integration in early time concepts. **Journal of Experimental Child Psychology, 37**(2), 262-70.

Reports results of a study in which boys and girls from kindergarten to second grade were asked to compare durations that differ in beginning times with those that differ in ending times. Possible sources of children's failure to integrate beginning and end points when comparing durations are discussed. Sex differences are discussed.

100. Majeres, R.L., & O'Toole, J. (1980). The effect of type of superordinate class and size of array on class-inclusion performance. **Journal of Genetic Psychology, 137**(2), 257-65.

Reports results of a study to determine performance variables explaining the developmentally late appearance of class-inclusion relative to conservation. Sex differences are discussed.

101. Martin, C.L., & Halverson, C.F., Jr. (1983). Gender constancy: a methodological and theoretical analysis. **Sex Roles: A Journal of Research, 9**(7), 775-90.

Verbal and perceptual tests of gender constancy were administered to four- to six-year olds. Majority of subjects answered questions as though referring to a "pretend" rather than "real" situation, which decreased scores of gender constancy on both tests.

102. Matheny, A.P., et al. (1980). Cognitive aspects of interests,

responsibilities and vocational goals in adolescence. **Adolescence, 15**(58), 301-11.

Reports results of interviews with mothers, coupled with adolescents' IQ scores, showing female adolescents' IQ scores were related to interests, responsibilities, and further education. Reports male adolescents' IQ scores were related to responsibilities and further education. Vocational goals provide some evidence of sex differences. Females are reported more reliable for a wide variety of responsibilities.

103. McCord, J.S., & Haynes, W.O. (1988). Discourse errors in students with learning disabilities and their normally achieving peers: molar versus molecular views. **Journal of Learning Disabilities, 21**(4), 237-43.

Compares twelve learning-disabled children, aged 8-11, with normal peers on various discourse errors. No significant quantitative differences are shown in the total number of discourse errors between the disabled and normal groups, but the errors were qualitatively different. Male subjects made significantly more errors than female subjects.

104. Miele, F. (1979). Cultural bias in the WISC. **Intelligence, 3**(2), 149-64.

Examines cultural bias in the Wechsler Intelligence Scale for Children. Results indicate no evidence of specific factors peculiar to blacks versus whites. Rank order of item difficulties are similar in both groups. Race differences are shown as differences in mental maturity rather than in test bias. Sex differences are discussed.

105. Perelle, I.B. (1979). Attention to stimulus presentation mode as a function of sex. **Journal of Psychology, 102**(2), 225-33.

Reports results of a study of attending behavior during the crossover period (12-13 years), when preferences shift from auditory to visual stimuli. Females switched their preferences significantly earlier than did males. Besides biological factors, sex differences are attributed to differential conditioning of attitudes, reinforcement, and discrimination regarding stimulus presentation mode.

106. Phipps, P.M. (1982). The LD learner is often a boy--why? **Academic Therapy, 17**(4), 425-30.

Reports results of a study in which the school records of 40 boys and 20 girls placed in special education programs (for learning disabled, educable retarded, or behavior disordered) were examined to compare reasons for referral and placement. Results indicate boys were more likely to be referred for behavior problems or behavior and academic problems.

107. Plomin, R., & Foch, T.T. (1981). Sex differences and individual differences. **Child Development, 52**(1), 383-5.

Examines sex differences and their relationship to individual differences for Maccoby and Jacklin's sex differences summaries, for a diverse set of measures of specific cognitive abilities (including verbal ability), and for objective personality assessments of school-age children.

108. Reynolds, C.R. (1980). Differential construct validity of intelligence as popularly measured: correlations of age with raw scores on the WISC-R for blacks, whites, males, and females. **Intelligence, 4**(4), 371-78.

Reports correlations of raw scores on WISC-R subtests and the verbal, performance, and full scale IQ scales with age separately for white and black males and females. The relationship between age and intelligence test performance was reported constant across race and sex, supporting construct validity of the WISC-R.

109. Saracho, O.N. (1984). Young children's academic achievement as a function of their cognitive styles. **Journal of Research and Development in Education, 18**(1), 44-50.

Examines the relationship between cognitive style and

academic performance of first- and third-grade students, focusing on differences in academic achievement. Sex differences are discussed.

110. Sex differences: right brain envy, (1979). **Science News, 115**(23), 375.

Reports results of spatial tests and analytical tasks indicating that girls tend to use the left hemisphere of the brain in processing all the tasks on spatial tasks and use it much more so than boys.

111. Smith, W.S., & Litman, C.I. (1979). Early adolescent girls' and boys' learning of a spatial visualization skill. **Science Education, 63**(5), 671-76.

Investigates the problem of whether a sex difference in spatial visualization ability exists among early adolescent students and whether the spatial visualization ability of boys and girls is affected differentially by instruction.

112. Smith, W.S., & Schroeder, C.K. (1981). Preadolescents' learning and retention of spatial visualization skill. **School Science and Mathematics, 81**(8), 705-09.

Investigates whether instruction in spatial visualization has different delayed effects on boys and girls, and whether girls and boys comparably retain spatial skills over time. Results indicate instruction for both sexes can improve spatial visualization abilities. No sex differences were found in learning or retention.

113. Smith, W.S., & Schroeder, C.K. (1979). Instruction of fourth grade girls and boys on spatial visualization. **Science Education, 63**(1), 61-66.

Investigates whether a difference in spatial ability existed among fourth grade boys and girls and whether their spatial ability would be differentially affected by instruction using the Spatial Visualization Abilities Test (SVAT) to measure performance. Sex differences are discussed.

114. Swan, M., & Jones, O.E. (1980). Comparison of students' perceptions of distance, weight, height, area, and temperature. **Science Education, 64**(3), 297-307.

Compares results of two 1971 studies, investigating Illinois childrens' percepts of several quantitative measures. Includes findings of improved ability in estimating intervals and quantities and in identifying ratios in conventional and metric units of measures. Establishes some relationships with ability and age, gender, and home.

115. Tamir, P. (1985). Meta-analysis of cognitive preferences and learning. **Journal of Research in Science Teaching, 22**(1), 1-17.

Presents meta-analysis of 54 articles and dissertations dealing with cognitive preferences. Information includes: test reliability; comparisons by country, grade level, gender, disciplines, and curricula; relationships between cognitive preferences and career orientation, science achievement, interest, and aptitude; and effect sizes. Results offer evidence supporting construct validity of cognitive preferences.

116. Tan-Willman, C., & Gutteridge, D. (1981). Creative thinking and moral reasoning of academically gifted secondary school adolescents. **Gifted Child Quarterly, 25**(4), 149-53.

Reports results of a study assessing creative thinking and moral reasoning of academically gifted male and female adolescents. Findings show some indications that relationship between creativity and moral reasoning differs across age, sex, and creativity subtests.

117. Townes, B.D., et al. (1980). Neuropsychological correlates of academic success among elementary school children. **Journal of Consulting and Clinical Psychology, 48**(6), 675-84.

Reports significant differences found between younger and older children on most neuropsychological tests. Girls are reported as superior to boys in verbal reasoning, language skills, and serial perceptual matching skills. Boys are shown as superior on tests of spatial memory and motor skills.

118. Treadgill-Sowder, J., et al. (1985). Cognitive variables and performance on mathematical story problems. **Journal of Experimental Education, 54**(1), 56-62.

Explores the relationships of certain cognitive variables to problem-solving performance. Cognitive restructuring, spatial ability, reading comprehension, and mathematical story problems tests presented in regular verbiage, low verbiage, and drawn formats were given to students in grades three through seven. Sex differences are discussed.

119. Treagust, D.F. (1980). Gender-related differences of adolescents in spatial representational thought. **Journal of Research in Science Teaching, 17**(2), 91-97.

Explores the relationship between performance and gender for junior- and senior-high students on six Piagetian-type tasks developed to measure infralogical spatial groupings. Results indicate a significant relationship between performance and gender on four tasks, in which males outscored females.

120. Vance, H. (1979). Sex differences on the WISC-R for retarded children and youth. **Psychology in the Schools, 16**(1), 27-31.

Investigates sex differences on the Wechsler Intelligence Scale for Children-Revised (WISC-R) subtests for retarded males and females who were matched for WISC-R Full Scale IQ's. Findings indicate a significant interaction effect between sex and subtest scores.

* Waber, D.P., et al. (1985). Physical maturation rate and cognitive performance in early adolescence: a longitudinal examination. **Developmental Psychology.** (Cited as entry 529.)

121. Wasik, B.H., et al. (1980). Basic concepts and conservation skill training in kindergarten children. **Perceptual and Motor Skills, 50**(1), 71-80.

Investigates the effects of basic concepts training on

conservation acquisition in kindergarten children. Sex differences are discussed.

122. Wavering, M.J., et al. (1986). Performance of students in grades six, nine, and twelve on five logical, spatial and formal tasks. **Journal of Research in Science Teaching, 23**(4), 321-33.

Examines performance on five logical, spatial, and formal tasks used to make inferences about the reasoning structures of middle and high school students. Findings include grade level differences in performance and sex differences in performance on one of the tasks.

123. Yore, L.D., et al. (1988). Exploration of the predictive and concurrent validity of a global measure of cognitive development for grade 1 reading, mathematics, and writing achievement. **Journal of Research and Development in Education, 21**(2), 62-69.

Investigates (1) whether a global cognitive development construct could effectively predict both concurrent and future grade 1 achievement in reading, writing, and mathematics, and (2) whether there are gender differences in the relationship between the construct and achievement. Sex differences are discussed.

Computers

124. Anderson, R.E., et al. (1984). Inequities in opportunities for computer literacy. **Computing Teacher, 11**(8), 10-12.

Discusses wealth, community size, region of the country, gender, and race as factors in access to microcomputer training in secondary schools in the United States, and presents statistics from various state and national surveys which indicate these variables play a determining role in computer literacy.

125. Cambre, M.A., & Cook, D.L. (1987). Measurement and remediation of computer anxiety. **Educational Technology, 7**(12), 15-20.

Reports results of study using precourse and postcourse questionnaires to identify computer anxiety. Subjects were a heterogeneous, voluntary population enrolled in a week-long introductory microcomputing course open to all ages as a community program. Relationships between computer anxiety and gender, age, and exposure to computers are discussed.

126. Chen, M. (1986). Gender and computers: the beneficial effects of experience on attitudes. **Journal of Educational Computing Research, 2**(3), 265-82.

Responses to a survey of high school students indicate male adolescents had greater total exposure to and more positive attitudes toward computers than females; there were fewer gender differences in enrollment in computer classes other than programming; and, when computer experience was controlled for, females showed similar levels of interest.

127. Cicchelli, T., & Baecher, R. (1985). Introducing microcomputers into the classroom: a study of teacher's concerns. **Journal of Educational Computing Research, 1**(1), 55-65.

Investigates reactions of elementary and secondary school teachers at the onset of implementing microcomputers in their schools. Results are discussed in terms of gender and teaching grade level differences, and the design of effective in-service education.

128. Collis, B. (1986). Research windows. **Computing Teacher, 13**(5), 46-47.

Presents the results of five studies: (1) new sight words for children who use computers; (2) immediate rewards for correct answers with computer assisted instruction; (3) importance of parental attitude and experience to student achievement with computers; (4) LOGO and adolescent females' mathematics achievement; and (5) competition versus cooperation for male and female mathematics achievement.

129. Collis, B. (1985). Sex differences in secondary school students' attitudes toward computers. **Computing Teacher, 12**(7), 33-36.

A study measuring eighth- and twelfth-grade students' attitudes toward computers. Sex and age differences, computer literacy course impact, and correlation of student attitudes toward computers and mathematics and science are assessed.

130. Collis, B. (1985). Sex-related differences in attitudes toward computers: implications for counselors. **School Counselor, 33**(2), 120-30.

Examines sex related differences in attitudes of secondary school students toward computers. Results indicate consistent sex differences in attitudes toward computers and mathematics, in attitudes and participation in computer study groups, and in attitudes and use of home computers.

131. Dalbey, J., & Linn, M.C. (1986). Cognitive consequences of programming: augmentations to basic instruction. **Journal of Educational Computing Research, 2**(1), 75-93.

Investigates academic achievement and higher cognitive skill development outcomes of a junior high school computer programming course in which two augmentations to traditional BASIC instruction were compared. A model for understanding learning outcomes is presented, suggesting ways to augment instruction to focus on higher cognitive skills. Sex differences are reported.

132. Demetrulias, D.M. (1985). Gender differences and computer use. **Educational Horizons, 63**(3), 133-35.

Assesses gender differences among students who use microcomputers in schools.

133. Eastman, S.T., & Krendl, K. (1987). Computers and gender: differential effects of electronic search on students' achievement and attitudes. Journal of Research and Development in Education, **20**(3), 41-48.

Reports results of a study of eighth-grade boys' and girls' attitudes toward and achievements in micro-searching using a microcomputer.

134. Enochs, L.G. (1984). The effect of computer instruction on general attitudes toward computers of fifth graders. **Journal of Computers in Mathematics and Science Teaching, 3**(3), 24-25.

Examines effects of beginning computer programming instruction, sex, and home computers on the attitudes of fifth-grade students. Results of this pilot study show higher attitudes following instruction and no differences between the sexes or between those who had computers and those who did not.

135. Enochs, L.G. (1986). General attitudes of middle school students toward computers. **Journal of Computers in Mathematics and Science Teaching, 5**(2), 56-57.

Reports results of a survey of the entire middle school population of a rural-suburban school district to determine the general attitudes of students toward computers. Findings are reported for differences in general attitudes toward computers between boys and girls, seventh and eighth-graders, and those who had computers and those who did not.

136. Fish, M.C., et al. (1986). The effect of equity strategies on girls' computer usage in school. **Computers in Human Behavior 2**(2) 127-34.

Provides results of an investigation of the effect of school-based equity strategies on seventh and eighth grade girls' voluntary computer usage. Girls in schools where the strategies were implemented used computers more than boys; the reverse was true in the control schools.

137. Griffin, B.L., et al. (1986). The counselor as a computer consultant: understanding children's attitudes toward computers. **Elementary School Guidance and Counseling, 20**(4), 246-49.

Examines elementary students' attitudes toward computers. Results indicate that sex, race, and socioeconomic differences are factors in developing attitudes.

138. Hodes, C.L. (1985) Relative effectiveness of corrective and non-corrective feedback in computer assisted instruction on learning and achievement. **Journal of Educational Technology Systems, 13**(4), 249-54.

Studies the impact of different feedback types on secondary school students in which treatment groups received either corrective or noncorrective feedback. Results indicate no significant difference between the groups' post-test scores, but when groups were redefined by gender, girls receiving non-corrective feedback scored lower than boys.

139. Kwan, S.K., et al. (1985). Gender differences and computing: students' assessment of societal influences. **Education and Computing**, **1**(3), 187-94.

Examines students' assessment of societal influences on their participation in computing. Gender differences in attitudes toward three factors are discussed: computing as male dominated, influence of significant others, and negative attitudes associated with computing and career aspirations. Students, especially females, rejected computing stereotypes.

140. Lindbeck, J.S., & Dambrot, F. (1986). Measurement and reduction of math and computer anxiety. **School Science and Mathematics**, **86**(7), 567-77.

Secondary teachers in a workshop on overcoming computer and math anxiety and secondary school students in a programming course were given measures of anxiety and achievement. Low mathematical ability and coursework were related to math and computer anxiety and negative attitudes. Attitudes improved for the teachers but not for students. Sex differences are reported.

141. Linn, M.C. (1985). Gender equity in computer learning environments. **Computers and the Social Sciences**, **1**(1), 19-27.

Characterizes gap between potential of computers in education and their performance in classrooms; documents differential participation of males and females in computer experiences and discusses contributory factors; describes two studies of how males and females respond to computer learning environments; suggests strategies to foster equitable outcomes in these environments.

* Louie, S., et al. (1985). Locus of control among computer-using school children: a report of a pilot study. **Journal of Educational Technology Systems.** (Cited as entry 668.)

142. Marshall, J.C. (1985). Computer attitudes and knowledge in rural settings. **Research in Rural Education, 2**(4), 155-58.

Reports results of a study of students and educators in rural settings concerning computer attitudes and knowledge. Educators and students had positive attitudes toward computers. Educators demonstrated significantly higher knowledge levels than students. Sex differences reported.

143. Moore, J.L. (1985). An empirical study of pupils' attitudes to computers and robots. **Journal of Computer Assisted Learning, 1**(2), 87-98.

Reports the result of using a Likert type questionnaire to assess seven scales of secondary pupils' attitudes toward computers and robotics (school, leisure, career, employment, social, threat, future) and investigates pupils' scores on functions by sex, general academic ability, course of study, and microcomputer experience.

144. Rhoads, C. (1986). The relationship between conditions and outcomes of microcomputer instruction. **Journal of Computers in Mathematics and Science Teaching, 5**(3), 48-50.

The effects of microcomputer instruction organization on three variables: (1) sex of student; (2) social arrangement of classroom; and (3) curricular presentation (high and low guidance) for algebra I

* Ross, S.M., & Anand, P.G. (1987). A computer-based strategy for personalizing verbal problems in teaching mathematics. **Educational Communication and Technology Journal.** (Cited as entry 369.)

145. Sanders, J.S. (1985). Making the computer neuter. **Computing Teacher, 12**(7), 23-27.

Summarizes findings of Computer Equity Training Project studies concerning female presence in computer magazines; home computer use variability by sex; student software evaluation; and influence on computer use of teacher gender, gender of other computer users, and work environment.

146. Sherwood, R.D., & Hasselbring, T. (1986). A comparison of student achievement across three methods of presentation of a computer-based science simulation. **Computers in the Schools, 2**(4), 43-50.

Investigates different presentation methods (pairs of students; entire class; and non-computer list game-type setting) of a computer-based science simulation to sixth-grade students to determine the most beneficial method for student achievement. Sex differences are reported.

147. Swadener, M., & Hannafin, M. (1987). Gender similarities and differences in sixth graders' attitudes toward computers: An exploratory study. **Educational Technology, 27**(1), 37-42.

Examines similarities and differences in computer related attitudes between sixth grade boys and girls of different mathematics achievement levels. Students' responses to questions about self-confidence in their computer abilities, the utility of computers, and general attitudes toward computers are reported and discussed.

148. Varner, I.I., & Grogg, P.M. (1988). Microcomputers and the writing process. **Journal of Business Communication, 25**(3), 69-78.

Assesses the microcomputer's effects on the process and quality of business writing, focusing on writing anxiety, computer anxiety, time spent in writing, writing quality, and the relationship of gender to these variables.

149. Vermette, S.M., et al. (1986). Attitudes of elementary school students and teachers toward computers in education. **Educational Technology, 26**(1), 41-47.

Reports negative reactions in personal, as opposed to

educational, issues in the teacher and student groups surveyed. Sex differences in attitudes are not reported although sex stereotyping is evident in both groups. Socialization issues are revealed in both groups relative to dehumanizing and isolating effects of computers.

Cultural and Cross-Cultural Studies

150. Albert, A.A., & Porter, J.R. (1986). Children's gender roles stereotypes: a comparison of the United States and South Africa. **Journal of Cross-Cultural Psychology, 17**(1), 45-65.

Compares the gender stereotypes of United States and South African white, urban middle class children. Focuses on the impact of age, sex, socioreligious background, and mother's employment status. Both groups made similar sex role assignments but cultural differences in gender stereotyping were observed.

151. Argulewicz, E.N., et al. (1985). Reliability and content validity of the Children's Anxiety Scale for Anglo-American and Mexican-American kindergarten children. **School Psychology Review, 14**(2), 236-38.

The Children's Anxiety Scale (CAS) was examined for bias in internal consistency reliability and item content for Anglo-American and Mexican-American kindergarten students. Results suggest equal test reliability for both groups, but also indicate caution must be exercised in interpreting CAS scores of young male children. Sex differences are discussed.

152. Benavot, A. (1989). Education, gender, and economic development: a cross-national study. **Sociology of Education, 62**(1), 14-32.

Examines effects of gender differences in educational expansion on national economic growth. Using cross-national data from 96 countries, authors report that in less-developed countries, educational expansion among primary school-age girls shows a stronger impact on long-term economic prosperity than educational expansion among primary school-age boys.

153. Browne, D.B. (1984). Scoring patterns among Native Americans of the Northern Plains. **White Cloud Journal, 3**(2), 3-16.

Wechsler Intelligence Scale for Children--Revised scoring patterns of Native American children at a Northern Plains boarding school were explored to identify characteristic cognitive processing strengths. Findings indicate greater strength than among standardization population in relational, holistic, right hemisphere information processing. Sex differences are discussed.

154. Davis, S.M., & Harris, M.B. (1982). Sexual knowledge, sexual interests, and sources of sexual information of rural and urban adolescents from three cultures. **Adolescence, 17**(66), 471-92.

Reports results of a study conducted of 288 adolescents surveying how their sources of sexual information, sexual interests, and actual knowledge were related to their sex, age, urban or rural residence, and ethnicity. Findings suggest demographic characteristics of students should be considered by persons interested in adolescent sexual knowledge.

155. Domino, G. (1981). Attitudes toward suicide among Mexican American and Anglo youth. **Hispanic Journal of Behavioral Sciences, 3**(4), 385-95.

Reports statistically significant differences between answers of 76 Anglo and 76 Mexican American youth on 35 of 100 opinion questionnaire items. Items center on religion, psychopathology, aggression-impulsivity, acceptability of suicide, the "cry for help" dimension, and emotional impact. Sex differences are discussed.

* Finn, J.D. (1980). Sex differences in educational outcomes: a cross-national study. **Sex Roles: A Journal of Research.** (Cited as entry 9.)

* Finn, J.D., et al. (1979). Sex differences in educational attainment: a cross-national perspective. **Harvard Educational Review.** (Cited as entry 10.)

* Fouad, N.A. (1988). The construct of career maturity in the United States and Israel. **Journal of Vocational Behavior.** (Cited as entry 50.)

156. Gaa, J.P., et al. (1986). Ethnic and gender concerns in sex-role identity: an illustration of problems in cross-cultural research. **Journal of Educational Equity and Leadership, 6**(2), 93-104.

Reports findings of three studies designed to examine patterns of masculinity and femininity in males and females separately both within and across three ethnic groups: Anglo, black, and Chicano. The first two studies examine identity patterns in adolescents, whereas the third examines the same patterns in elementary school students.

157. Gaa, J.P., et al. (1981). Domain-specific locus of control orientations of Anglo, black, and Chicano adolescents. **Journal of Psychology, 107**(2), 185-91.

Reports results of a study using Locus of Control in Three Achievement Domains (LOCITAD), to examine differences in Anglo, black, and Chicano high school students with respect to success and failure in three domains--intellectual, social, and physical. Sex differences are discussed.

158. Greaney, V., & Neuman, S.B. (1983). Young people's views of the functions of reading: a cross-cultural perspective. **Reading Teacher**, **37**(2), 158-63.

Explores the reading activities of students in grades three, five, and eight in Ireland and the United States through the use of a functions of reading scale. Results show the patterns of relationships between the variables in the Scale to be consistent across cultures and grade levels. Sex differences are discussed.

* Guida, F.V., & Ludlow, L.H. (1989). A cross-cultural study of test anxiety. **Journal of Cross-Cultural Psychology.** (Cited as entry 769.)

* Hanna, G. (1989). Mathematics achievement of girls and boys in grade eight: results from twenty countries. **Educational Studies in Mathematics.** (Cited as entry 347.)

159. Heston, M., et al. (1986). Reliability of selected measures of movement control and force production on children four through ten years of age. **Physical Educator, 43**(4), 195-97.

Reports the results of a study to establish tentative reliability estimates for movement control and force production tasks as the initial phase of a cross-cultural motor-performance study. Boys and girls for each of seven age groups (ages four through ten) performed four specific tasks.

160. Howell, F.M., & Frese, W. (1979). Race, sex, and aspirations: evidence for the 'race convergence' hypothesis. **Sociology of Education, 52**(1), 34-46.

Describes research testing the 'race convergence' hypothesis for high school students of low socioeconomic background. Findings show that many race differentials in the aspiration-formation process disappear at this level. Sex differences are discussed.

161. Kishta, M.A. (1979). Proportional and combinatorial reasoning in two cultures. **Journal of Research in Science Teaching, 16**(5), 439-43.

Discusses influences of a student's gender, grade level, country of origin, and urban/rural environment in performance of proportional and combinatorial Piagetian tasks.

162. Lin, R. (1987). A profile of reservation Indian high school girls. **Journal of American Indian Education, 26**(2), 18-28.

Reports results of a comparison of American Indian girls and boys on a reservation to white girls, showing Indian girls faced the most difficult problems. Findings show Indian girls may have distant relationships with their parents, especially their fathers. They may be less social, less trusting and more likely to want to commit suicide.

163. Littrell, J.M., & Littrell, M.A. (1982). American Indian and Caucasian students' preferences for counselors: effects of counselor dress and sex. **Journal of Counseling Psychology, 29**(1), 48-57.

Examines effects of two nonverbal cues, counselor's dress and sex, on high school students' preferences for counselors. Results of the multivariate analysis of variance show students' preferences for counselors varied with counselors' sex and dress, type of concern, and race of students.

* London, C.B.G., & Griffith, A.R. (1981). Inner-city teachers and school community relations. **Urban Education.** (Cited as entry 568.)

164. Machida, S. (1986). Teacher accuracy in decoding nonverbal indicants of comprehension and noncomprehension in Anglo- and Mexican-American children. **Journal of Educational Psychology, 78**(6), 454-64.

The degree to which Anglo- and Mexican-American first-grade teachers can accurately decode non-verbal indicants of comprehension and noncomprehension was examined. Teachers perceived boys as understanding more than girls. Slight cultural differences were found in children's behavior, but it did not affect teachers' interpretation.

* Maccoby, E.E., & Jacklin, C.N. (1980). Sex differences in aggression: a rejoinder and reprise. **Child Development.** (Cited as entry 472.)

* Miele, F. (1979). Cultural bias in the WISC. **Intelligence.** (Cited as entry 104.)

* Miura, I.T., & Okamoto, Y. (1989). Comparisons of U.S. and Japanese first graders' cognitive representation of number and understanding of place value. **Journal of Educational Psychology.** (Cited as entry 360.)

* Reynolds, C.R. (1980). Differential construct validity of intelligence as popularly measured: correlations of age with raw scores on the WISC-R for blacks, whites, males, and females. **Intelligence.** (Cited as entry 108.)

165. Rivas, M. (1984). Cognitive styles of Mexican-American and Anglo-American five, eight, and ten-year-old boys and girls. **Texas Tech Journal of Education, 11**(1), 67-76.

Mexican-American and Anglo-American children were studied to observe how their culture influences their learning style. Findings indicate no significant cultural difference in dimensions of cognitive style for these two groups. Sex differences are discussed.

166. Safir, M.P. (1986). The effects of nature or of nurture on sex differences in intellectual functioning: Israeli findings. **Sex Roles: A Journal of Research, 14**(11-12), 581-90.

Contrasts results of studies examining sex differences in intellectual functioning in the U.S. and Israel, in cities and on kibbutzes. Findings indicate cross-cultural and intracultural influences challenge the validity of theories that suggest a biological basis for sex differences in intellectual abilities.

167. Stigler, J.W., et al. (1985). The self-perception of competence by Chinese children. **Child Development, 56**(5), 1259-70.

Harter's Perceived Competence Scale for Children was administered to Taiwanese fifth graders; results were compared with those from American samples. Cultural differences are reported. Results among Chinese replicate the measures' factorial validity and, across the two groups, indicate a high correlation between perceived cognitive competence and actual achievement in school. Sex differences are discussed.

* Tamir, P. (1985). Meta-analysis of cognitive preferences and learning. **Journal of Research in Science Teaching.** (Cited as entry 115.)

168. Thomas, B.J. (1987). Comparison of rural kindergarten report card grades. **Journal of American Indian Education, 26**(2), 7-17.

Reports results of a study of grades for all kindergarten children in a rural midwestern town near an American Indian reservation. Examines the variables of gender, class time, parent involvement, ethnicity, socioeconomic status, and family style.

169. Velasco-Barraza, C.R., & Muller, D. (1982). Development of self-concept in Chilean, Mexican, and United States school children. **Journal of Psychology, 110**(1), 21-30.

Results of this study suggest there are substantial similarities in development across national groups; there is a tendency for differences between national groups to decrease as grade level increases.

170. Vernon, S.W., & Roberts, R.E. (1985). A comparison of Anglos and Mexican Americans on selected measures of social support. **Hispanic Journal of Behavioral Sciences**, 7(4), 381-99.

Differences between Anglos and Mexican Americans are examined for three measures of social support--organizational membership, contact with friends and relatives, and sources of socioemotional and instrumental aid. Most initial ethnic differences disappeared when the effects of age, gender, education, income, and marital status were controlled.

Delinquent Youth | Drug and Alcohol Problems | Behavior Problems

171. Alvord, J.B. (1979). Male/female dynamics and student discipline. **NASSP Bulletin, 63**(428), 55-58.

Reports results of a study showing male teachers refer male students for disciplinary action 2.5 times more often than they refer female students. Female teachers refer boys 1.3 times more often. Findings show male and female staff refer girls in nearly the same number.

172. Atkinson, D.R., & Dorsey, M.F. (1979). The effects of counseling for conformity or social change on perceived counselor credibility. **Journal of Counseling Services, 3**(1), 12-17.

Reports results of a study to determine if high school students would rate the counselor's credibility differently when the counselor functioned as an agent of social change rather than as an agent of social conformity. Females tended to rate the conformity role highest.

173. Bear, G.G. (1989). Sociomoral reasoning and antisocial behaviors among normal sixth graders. **Merrill-Palmer Quarterly, 35**(2), 181-96.

Reports results of a study of 77 sixth-graders showing sociomoral reasoning correlating with both socialized and unsocialized aggressive behaviors, but not with attention problems, anxiety-withdrawal, or motor tension without aggression. A relationship between maturity of sociomoral reasoning and self-reported antisocial behavior among boys only is reported.

174. Blyth, D.A., et al. (1980). Another look at school crime: student as victim. **Youth and Society, 11**(3), 369-88.

Reports results of a study showing no significant sex and race differences found between victims and nonvictims of crime in K-8 schools. However, in junior highs, whites and males were most likely to be victimized. Social-psychological consequences of victimization included lowered self-esteem and perception of anonymity, especially among victims in white junior highs.

175. Boldizar, J.P., et al. (1989). Outcome values and aggression. **Child Development, 60**(3), 571-79.

Reports results of a study testing hypothesis that aggressive children attach more value to rewarding outcomes of aggression and less to negative outcomes than do nonaggressive children. Sex differences in outcome values are discussed.

176. Brodzinsky, D.M., et al. (1979). Sex differences in children's expression and control of fantasy and overt aggression. **Child Development, 50**(2), 372-79.

Reports results of a study of fifth-grade boys and girls presented with a TAT-like projective test to measure fantasy aggression and controls over aggression. Overt peer-oriented aggression was measured by peer and teacher ratings.

177. Bruno, J.E., & Doscher, L. (1979). Patterns of drug use among Mexican-American potential school dropouts. **Journal of Drug Education, 9**(1), 1-10.

Reports results of a study of a sample of Mexican-American students identified as potential dropouts finding drug use widespread. Findings show (1) use of cigarettes, marijuana, and alcohol by majority of students, (2) students do not think general drug use causes social problems. Girls' attitudes differ from boys'.

178. Burdsal, C., & Force, R.C. (1983). An examination of counselor ratings of behavior problem youth in an early stage, community-based intervention program. **Journal of Clinical Psychology, 39**(3), 353-60.

Explores counselor ratings of 10- to 13-year-old students in three therapeutic camping trips. Results indicate a significant difference between boys and girls from third-trip comparisons on unstructured dependence. Reliable counselor ratings are shown. Boys were perceived by counselors to change, while girls did not.

179. Clemens, P.W., & Rust, J.O. (1979). Factors in adolescent rebellious feelings. **Adolescence, 14**(53), 159-73.

Reports results of a study examining 15- and 16-year-old youths' feelings of anomie and rebellion in relation to family and situational factors. Only parents' formal education level and subjects' approval of the way they were being reared correlated significantly with comparable adolescent scores on the Anomie and Rebellion Scales. Sex differences are discussed.

180. Cotten-Huston, A.L. (1982). Student interests and attitude change toward drug educators as a function of sex and role interaction. **Journal of Drug Education, 12**(1), 43-54.

Reports results of a study focused on recorded tapes and sex-role interaction of 12 sessions on drug abuse. Subjects were 247 seventh-grade males and females. Male and female communicators made two presentations with roles rotated according to ex-addict/learned specialist. Results indicate female and male students were influenced most by female specialist communicators.

181. Cullinan, D., et al. (1981). School behavior problems of learning disabled and normal girls and boys. **Learning Disability Quarterly, 4**(2), 163-69.

Reports results of teacher ratings of learning disabled and normal 7-12 year olds on the Behavior Problem Checklist. Ratings show school behavior problems varied by sex and pupil category.

182. Cullinan, D., et al. (1984). Teachers' ratings of students' behaviors: what constitutes behavior disorders in schools? **Behavioral Disorders, 10**(1), 9-19.

Behaviorally disordered and nonhandicapped students of three age levels were assessed for adjustment problems, using a teacher-completed checklist. Results show that on most checklist items significantly more behaviorally disordered students experienced problems than nonhandicapped students. Among the behaviorally disordered students, there were few differences between sexes and age.

183. DeJong, W. (1987). A short-term evaluation of Project DARE (Drug Abuse Resistance Education): preliminary indications of effectiveness. **Journal of Drug Education, 17**(4), 279-94.

Assesses impact of Project DARE (Drug Abuse Resistance Education) on knowledge, attitudes, and self-reported behavior of seventh graders who received DARE curriculum in sixth grade. Compared to controls, DARE students reported significantly lower use of alcohol, cigarettes, and other drugs. Findings are especially strong for boys.

184. Dodson, P.K., & Evans, E.D. (1985). A developmental study of school theft. **Adolescence, 20**(79), 509-23.

Students in grades 4 through 8 and 10 completed questionnaires measuring perceptions of school theft incidence and seriousness, personal responsibility for correcting theft, causal attributions of theft, and perceived consequences of thievery. Main grade effect was observed for personal responsibility and consequences, but represented counter directions. Eighth graders reported highest theft incidence; females prescribed harsher penalties for theft.

185. Downs, W.R. (1985). Using panel data to examine sex differences in causal relationships among adolescent

alcohol use, norms, and peer alcohol use. **Journal of Youth and Adolescence, 14**(6), 469-86.

Reports results of the study of longitudinal data and multiple regression of follow-up data to identify direction of causality among adolescent alcohol use, normative structure toward alcohol, and peer alcohol use. Separate regressions were performed on male and female respondents.

186. Edelbrock, C., & Achenback, T.M. (1980). A topology of child behavior profile patterns: distribution and correlates for disturbed children aged 6-16. **Journal of Abnormal Child Psychology, 8**(4), 441-70.

Reports results of a study using hierarchical cluster analysis from scores on the Child Behavior Profile to identify reliable profile patterns characterizing clinically referred boys and girls.

187. Emery, R.E., & O'Leary, K.D. (1982). Children's perceptions of marital discord and behavior problems of boys and girls. **Journal of Abnormal Child Psychology, 10**(1), 11-24.

Reports results of a study of 50 behavior problem children showing that (1) marital discord, as predicted, was most strongly related to conduct problems in boys, (2) boys and girls perceived parental marital discord with equal and moderate accuracy, and (3) children's feelings of nonacceptance were not significantly related to ratings of marital discord.

188. Estep, L.E., et al. (1980). Teacher pupil control ideology and behavior as predictors of classroom robustness. **High School Journal, 63**(4), 155-59.

Reports results of a study hypothesizing that confrontations between a strict teacher and misbehaving students would add drama and robustness to the classroom. The hypothesis was rejected; humanistic control behavior related to high robustness. Sex differences are discussed.

189. Figueira-McDonough, J. (1986). School context, gender, and delinquency. **Journal of Youth and Adolescence, 15**(1), 79-98.

Two high schools serving the same community are compared in order to examine how control/strain variables predict delinquency in two contexts. The school context characterized by a broader definition of success, more specialized discipline, and predictable supervision was found to produce lower levels of delinquency for both genders.

190. French, D.C., & Waas, G.A. (1985). Behavior problems of peer-neglected and peer-rejected elementary-age children: parent and teacher perspectives. **Child Development,** 56(1), 246-52.

Presents standardized parent and teacher behavior ratings of neglected and rejected 8- to 11-year-old boys and girls. No age or sex differences were found. Rejected children were found to exhibit more behavior problems on both scales than neglected, popular, or average children.

191. Gibbons, S., et al. (1986). Patterns of alcohol use among rural and small-town adolescents. **Adolescence, 21**(84), 885-900.

Examines patterns of rural adolescent alcohol use and factors associated with such use. Gender and grade in school are significant predictors of alcohol use for age at first drink, frequency of drinking, amount of drinking, and a composite heavy drinking index.

192. Gottfredson, D.C. (1985). Youth employment, crime, and schooling: a longitudinal study of a national sample. **Developmental Psychology, 21**(3), 419-32.

Data from a national study of delinquency prevention programs were used to examine the effect of teenage employment on delinquent behavior in preadolescents and adolescents. Models examined suggest working decreases school attendance and dependence on parents for some subgroups, but these effects are not translated into increases in delinquency. Sex differences are discussed.

193. Haviland, J.M. (1979). Teachers' and students' beliefs about punishment. **Journal of Educational Psychology, 71**(4), 563-70.

Reports results of two interviews with first-, third-, and fifth-grade children and their teachers assessing developing relationship between teachers' and students' beliefs about punishment. Teachers with more punitive beliefs had students whose beliefs were more punitive when compared with students whose teachers had less punitive beliefs. Sex differences are discussed.

194. Hicks, R.A., et al. (1980). Change in the classroom deportment of children following change from daylight saving time. **Perceptual and Motor Skills, 51**(1), 101-02.

Reports results of a study asking whether disruption in circadian rhythms alters behavior. Deportment of third grade students was rated by the teacher before and after the fall change from daylight savings time. Deportment of boys improved significantly while deportment of girls was significantly disrupted.

195. Huba, G.J., et al. (1981). Is coca paste currently a drug of abuse among high school students? **Journal of Drug Education, 11**(3), 205-12.

Studies use of the drug coca paste by high school students in Los Angeles. Of 11th- and 12th-grade males four claimed to have recently used coca paste, and of females, five reported using the drug.

196. Huffine, S., et al. (1979). Teacher responses to contextually specific sex type behaviors in kindergarten children. **Educational Research Quarterly, 4**(2), 29-35.

Reports results of a study showing kindergarten teachers likely to discipline when boys were verbally disruptive and when girls demonstrated aggressive behaviors. Teachers were physical when responding to boys' disruptions and used verbal and nonverbal behaviors when responding to girls' disruptive behaviors. Girls' questions received longer teacher responses.

197. Just, D.A. (1985). Delinquent youth and employment: the mandate for specialized academic and vocational training. **Journal for Vocational Special Needs Education, 7**(3), 11-16, 34.

The relationships between delinquent behavior and labor market experiences of teenagers are examined in this study. Variables include incidence of self-reported delinquent behavior, gender, race, age, suspension from school, and current residence. Findings and the implications for educational policy are examined.

198. Just, D.A. (1985). The relationship between delinquent behavior and work values of non-institutionalized youth. **Journal of Correctional Education, 36**(4), 148-54.

Reports results of a study conducted to determine whether the work values of delinquent youth differ from those of other youth, and if so, how. Sex differences are discussed.

* Kaufman, A.S., et al. (1979). Dimensions of problem behaviors of emotionally disturbed children as seen by their parents and teachers. **Psychology in the Schools.** (Cited as entry 233.)

199. Kedar-Voivodas, G., & Tannenbaum, A.J. (1979). Teachers' attitudes toward young deviant children. **Journal of Educational Psychology, 71**(6), 800-08.

Investigates impact of information about behaviors, labels, psychotherapy and sex of hypothetical pupils on teachers' expectations of present and future school functioning. Sex differences are discussed.

200. Keyes, S., & Block, J. (1984). Prevalence and patterns of substance use among early adolescents. **Journal of Youth and Adolescence, 13**(1), 1-14.

Data on adolescents (age 14) from a longitudinal study of ego and cognitive development in the San Francisco East Bay area is used to assess the frequency, context, and initiation of uses of alcohol, tobacco, and "harder" drugs. Comparisons are made with 1981 national statistics on high school seniors. Sex differences are discussed.

201. Lancelotta, G.X., & Vaughn, S.L. (1989). Relation between types of aggression and sociometric status: peer and teacher perceptions. **Journal of Educational Psychology, 81**(1), 86-90.

Reports results of a study involving male and female third and fourth graders analyzing relation between five subtypes of aggressive behavior and sociometric status as assessed by ratings by peers and by teachers. Social status and gender are shown as significantly related to type of aggression exhibited.

202. Ludwig, G., & Cullinan, D. (1984). Behavior problems of gifted and nongifted elementary school girls and boys. **Gifted Child Quarterly, 28**(1), 37-39.

Compares personal and social adjustment of gifted and nongifted elementary school students. Findings show gifted students evidenced fewer behavior problems. Boys of both gifted and nongifted groups demonstrated greater conduct disorder problems.

203. McCarthy, W.J., et al. (1986). Smokeless tobacco use among adolescents: demographic differences, other substance use, and psychological correlates. **Journal of Drug Education, 16**(4), 383-402.

Reports the results of a survey of seventh, ninth, and eleventh graders on smokeless tobacco and other substance use. Examines patterns of smokeless tobacco use relative to other drug use, particularly cigarette smoking. Data supports view that recent increases in use of smokeless tobacco are related to male tobacco users' belief that smokeless tobacco is less harmful to physical health than cigarette smoking. Sex differences are discussed.

204. McClary, S.A., & Lubin, B. (1985). Effects of type of examiner,sex, and year in school on self report of drug use by high school students. **Journal of Drug Education, 15**(1), 49-55.

Reports results of a study that manipulates three types of examiners and four types of data in order to study the examiner effect on self-reports of drug use by students. Analysis reveals that type of examiner, sex, and year in school had a significant three way interaction affecting self-reports of drug use.

205. McIntosh, W.A. (1979). Age and drug use by rural and urban adolescents. **Journal of Drug Education, 9**(2), 129-43.

Assesses importance of age in determining use of conventional and illicit drugs among secondary school students in Texas. Age-drug use relationships are examined for sex, age, and residence of respondents. Findings show rural students' use of deviant drugs exceeded that of urban students. Sex differences are discussed.

206. Messer, S.B., & Brodzinsky, D.M. (1979). The relation of conceptual tempo to aggression and its control. **Child Development, 50**(3), 758-66.

Fifth-grade boys and girls were administered the Matching Familiar Figures Test and a projective measure of fantasy aggression and its control. They were also rated sociometrically by peers and teachers on physical, verbal, and indirect forms of overt aggression. Results indicate conceptual tempo was related to aggression and its control. Sex differences are discussed.

207. Milgram, G.G., & Pandina, R.J. (1981). Educational implications of adolescent substance use. **Journal of Alcohol and Drug Education, 26**(3), 13-22.

Explores the educational implications of a specific survey on the nature and extent of adolescent alcohol and drug use. Sex differences are discussed.

208. Moore, L.P., et al. (1982). Conditioning children's attitudes toward alcohol, smoking and drugs. **Journal of Experimental Education, 50**(3), 154-58.

Reports results of a study with elementary and secondary school students in which classical conditioning procedures were used to change attitudes and choice of social behavior associated with drinking, smoking, and drugs. Findings show the experimental group expressed more negative attitudes toward smoking and drinking and chose the use of drugs less frequently. Sex differences are discussed.

209. Moskowitz, J.M., et al. (1984). The effects of drug education at follow-up. **Journal of Alcohol and Drug Education, 30**(1), 45-49.

Presents a one-year follow-up of a drug education course for junior high school students. Analyses of variance and covariance were performed on class-level data collected at follow-up. None of the short-term effects of the course sustained. Sex differences are discussed.

210. Moskowitz, J.M., et al. (1984). An experimental evaluation of a drug education course. **Journal of drug education, 14**(1), 9-22.

Evaluates a drug education course for junior high school students which included decision-making skills, assertiveness training, and drug information and alternatives. Comparison of experimental and control groups shows the course had no significant effect on girls and only a few effects on boys.

211. Myers, V. (1979). Interaction in the research interview and drug-related disclosures among respondents. **Journal of Drug Education, 9**(2), 105-17.

Reports results of a study in which interviewers and respondents judged interview interactions during a survey of drug-related sentiments. Findings show pronounced variability in interviewer-respondent judgments in unanticipated ways related to gender, role, and ethnicity of participants.

212. Pascale, P.J., et al. (1985). Regional trends and sex differences of drug use and attitudes of high school students in Northeast Ohio 1977-1983. **Journal of Drug Education, 15**(3), 241-51.

Presents trend analyses of data collected from three large scale surveys of eleventh grade students in Northeast Ohio using the same drug use and attitudes instrument between 1977 and 1983. Frequency of usage, reason for taking drugs, perceived harmfulness, age of first experimentation with drugs, and sex differences are analyzed.

213. Peretti, P.O., et al. (1984). Affect of parental rejection on negative attention-seeking classroom behaviors. **Education, 104**(3), 313-17.

Student questionnaires and teacher interviews provided data on Chicago third graders to determine the affect of parental rejection on negative attention-seeking classroom behaviors, what particular parent might be more rejecting, and what specific negative attention-seeking behaviors might be overtly demonstrated in the classroom by sex of subject.

214. Perry, D.G., et al. (1986). Cognitive social mediators of aggression. **Child Development, 57**(3), 700-11.

Explores links between aggression in elementary school children and their perceptions of self-efficacy as well as their response-outcome expectancies. Sex differences are discussed.

215. Rohrkemper, M. (1985). Individual differences in students' perceptions of routine classroom events. **Journal of Educational Psychology, 77**(1), 29-44.

Reports results of a study in which elementary school students, differing in classroom adjustment, were presented with three written vignettes portraying inappropriate student behavior. Students' predictions of their teacher's motivation and responses to the vignette characters, as well as their own response and understanding, were analyzed for differences by grade, sex, and classroom adjustment.

216. Sheppard, M.A., & Mitchell, M. (1986). Young people's view of alcohol and its use. **Journal of Alcohol and Drug Education, 31**(2), 1-7.

Examines children's posters about alcohol and its effect, to gain insight into children's attitudes and values toward alcohol. Results focus upon themes and age and sex differences. Implications for alcohol education programs are given.

217. Shover, N., et al. (1979). Gender roles and delinquency. **Social Forces, 58**(1), 162-75.

The masculinity theory and the theory of opportunity and social controls are used comparatively to explain the different rates of delinquency for boys and girls. Of the two theories, the opportunity and controls theory is found to have considerably more empirical support.

218. Sommer, B. (1985). What's different about truants? A comparison study of eighth-graders. **Journal of Youth and Adolescence, 14**(5), 411-22.

Differences and similarities between eighth-grade truants

and non-truants--matched for age, grade, gender, and ethnicity--were explored on four dimensions: family variables, friendship patterns and interests, behavior and attitudes toward school, and cognitive factors including academic ability and achievement.

* Stern, M., et al. (1984). Father absence and adolescent "problem behaviors": alcohol consumption, drug use and sexual activity. **Adolescence.** (Cited as entry 246.)

219. Trahan, D., & Stricklin, A. (1979). Bender-Gestalt Emotional Indicators and acting-out behavior in young children. **Journal of Personality Assessment, 43**(4), 365-75.

Investigates the relationship between 15 emotional indicators on the Bender Gestalt Test and the acting out behavior of children, ages 5 to 12, as rated by their teachers. Questions the use of the Bender as a projective measure. Sex differences are discussed.

220. Walberg, H.J., & Heise, K. (1979). The distribution of misbehavior: a research note. **Psychology in the Schools, 16**(2), 306-08.

Reports findings from school records of the numbers of disciplinary referrals to the principal's office for 202 boys and 202 girls from a middle-class, suburban junior high school.

221. Welte, J.W., & Barnes, G.M. (1987). Youthful smoking: patterns and relationships to alcohol and other drug use. **Journal of Adolescence, 10**(4), 327-40.

Examines smoking patterns in junior and senior high school students. Findings show smoking more prevalent among girls than boys, and among whites more than members of minority groups.

222. Winfree, L.T., Jr., et al. (1981). The initiation and avoidance of drugs by adolescents in the southwest. **Journal of Drug Education, 11**(4), 327-40.

Investigates the reasons cited for using drugs. Examines

characteristics of abstainers and their reasons for non-use and compares this group with former drug users. Sex differences are discussed.

223. Wooldridge, P., & Richman, C.L. (1985). Teachers' choice of punishment as a function of student's gender, age, race, and IQ level. **Journal of School Psychology, 23**(1), 19-29.

Examines whether teachers treat students differently according to various characteristics. Southern white female teachers recommend punishment for a hypothetical student in fighting, stealing, and cheating situations. Results reveal that teachers recommend more severe punishment for males than for females and for white males more than for black males.

224. Zingraff, M.T. (1980). Inmate assimilation: a comparison of male and female delinquents. **Criminal Justice and Behavior,** 7(3), 275-92.

Data from two juvenile correctional facilities indicate that the deprivation model is a better predictor of adaptation to confinement for males than is the importation model. For females, variables from both deprivation and importation models show significant impact.

Family Settings

225. Benin, M.H., & Johnson, D.R. (1984). Sibling similarities in educational attainment: a comparison of like-sex and cross-sex sibling pairs. **Sociology of Education, 57**(1), 11-21.

Tests hypothesis that the amount of educational resemblance of siblings differs across the sex combinations of pairs. Educational resemblance is greatest among older brother-younger brother pairs and smallest among older sister-younger sister pairs.

226. Brody, G.H., et al. (1985). Role relationships and behavior between preschool-aged and school-aged sibling pairs. **Developmental Psychology, 21**(1), 124-29.

Reports results of a study that observed role relationships and behaviors that characterize interactions of preschool-aged sibling pairs and school-aged sibling pairs. Seven roles were observed: teacher, learner, manager, managee, helper, helpee, and observer. Instances of prosocial and agonistic behavior were also observed in unstructured naturalistic activities at home. Sex differences are discussed.

227. deTurck, M.A., & Miller, G.R. (1983). Adolescent perceptions of parental persuasive message strategies. **Journal of Marriage and the Family, 45**(3), 543-22.

Reports results of a survey of adolescents to investigate adolescent perceptions of parental persuasive communication. Argues that adolescents base their attributions of parental power on their parents' attempts to control their behavior. Results indicate that adolescents' age and gender and communicative context affect how they perceive parental persuasive message strategies. Sex differences are discussed.

228. Dix, T., and Grusec, J.E. (1983). Parental influence techniques: an attributional analysis. **Child Development, 54**(3), 545-52.

Examines whether parents of children ages 5 through 13 are able to recognize the impact various socialization techniques have on their child's interpretations of prosocial behavior. Also, investigates parents' beliefs about causal attributions made by their children. Sex differences are discussed.

229. Gilbert, L.A., et al. (1982). Perceptions of parental role responsibilities: differences between mothers and fathers. **Family Relations, 31**(2), 261-69.

Investigates fathers' influence on socialization of children and how it may differ from that of mothers. Parents responded to seven scales concerning parental role responsibilities. Fathers and mothers reported high agreement as to major parental role responsibilities for a male child, less agreement occurred for female children.

230. Griffore, R.J., & Schweitzer, J.H. (1983). Child-parent social attitude relationships. **Psychology: A Quarterly Journal of Human Behavior, 20**(1), 9-13.

Investigates degree to which children's racial attitudes were related to their parents' racial attitudes. Results show children's attitudes positively associated with parents' attitudes regardless of the parent's sex or child's age. Beginning at about age 12, girls' attitudes became more liberal and boys' attitudes more conservative.

* Hart, E.J., & Behr, M.T. (1980). The effects of educational intervention & parental support on dental health. **Journal of School Health.** (Cited as entry 509.)

231. Hoffman, L.W. (1980). The effects of maternal employment on

the academic attitudes and performance of school-aged children. **School Psychology Review, 9**(4), 319-35.

A review of research concentrating on the effects of maternal employment on the academic attitudes and performance of children in elementary and secondary schools. Related research is reviewed, hypotheses about the relationship are developed, and research needs are indicated. Sex differences are discussed.

232. Holloway, S.D. (1986). The relationship of mothers' beliefs to children's mathematics achievement: some effects of sex differences. **Merrill-Palmer Quarterly, 32**(3), 231-50.

Investigates whether mothers' beliefs about achievement were related to their seventh grade children's sex differences, and the association between these beliefs and their children's performance in mathematics.

233. Kaufman, A.S., et al. (1979). Dimensions of problem behaviors of emotionally disturbed children as seen by their parents and teachers. **Psychology in the Schools, 16**(2), 207-17.

Compares the factor structure of parents' and teachers' ratings of children's behavior problems. Data is analyzed for a heterogeneous group of 194 emotionally disturbed boys and girls aged 3-13 years. Sex differences are discussed.

234. Kinard, E.M., & Reinherz, H. (1987). School aptitude and achievement in children of adolescent mothers. **Journal of Youth and Adolescence, 16**(1), 69-87.

Data from a longitudinal study was used to study the effects of adolescent child bearing on the academic aptitude and achievement of fourth graders. Birth order, family structure, and maternal education were controlled. Results showed that maternal education had a greater impact on the outcome measures than did maternal age. Sex differences are discussed.

235. Lietz, J.J. (1981). Unannounced desegregation in an all-

volunteer summer school: sex, grade, and ethnic attendance patterns. **Educational Research Quarterly, 6**, 77-85.

Reports results of a study investigating whether parent desire to avoid racial mixing resulted in school avoidance, independent of other commonly cited explanations for enrollment and attendance patterns in newly desegregated schools. Sex differences are discussed.

236. Melson, G.F., et al. (1986). Children's ideas about infants and their care. **Child Development, 57**(6), 1519-27.

Examines effects of age, sex, and sibling status on children's ideas about infants and infant care. The sample consisted of preschoolers and second graders, divided evenly by sex. Older children with siblings were more knowledgeable than either their only-child peers or younger children.

237. Mensah, K.L., et al. (1983). Parent education needs of secondary students. **Family Relations, 32**(2), 181-89.

Assesses parent education needs of secondary students as a basis for the development of parent education programs. Data were collected by administering the Parent Information Inventory. Students expressed strongest needs in planning and decision making, parenting and adolescent social development. Significant sex and age differences were found.

238. Mercier, J.M., & Hughes, R.P. (1981). Attitudes of selected secondary students toward family planning education. **Home Economics Research Journal, 10**(2), 127-36.

Examines possible relationships of attitudes of secondary students toward family planning education and selected variables of sex, age, religion, occupation of mother, and occupation of father. Findings indicate students are supportive of family planning education although females generally favored such education more than males.

239. Nunn, G.D., et al. (1983). Perceptions of personal and familial adjustment by children from intact, single-parent, and

reconstituted families. **Psychology in the Schools, 20**(2), 166-74.

Investigates children's personal and familial adjustment as a function of familial configuration and gender. Results reveal less positive adjustment among children from divorced families. Males appeared to be favorably affected within the single-parent configuration, while females were more favorably adjusted within the reconstituted family.

240. Nurmi, J. (1987) Age, sex, social class, and quality of family interaction as determinants of adolescents' future orientation: a developmental task interpretation. **Adolescence, 22**(88), 977-91.

Reports that subjects' future aims and fears show close relation to developmental tasks.

* Perretti, P.O., et al. (1984). Affect of parental rejection on negative attention-seeking classroom behaviors. **Education.** (Cited as entry 213.)

241. Peterson, G.W., et al. (1982). Social placement of adolescents: sex-role influences on family decisions regarding the careers of youth. **Journal of Marriage and the Family, 44**(3), 647-58.

Investigates whether families tend to make decisions that provide differential support for career goals of male and female offspring and examines choices of members about "appropriate" career goals for adolescent females. Results indicate family decisions favored career goals of adolescent males over adolescent females.

242. Ponzetti, J.J., Jr., & Folkrod, A.N. (1989). Grandchildren's perceptions of their relationships with their grandparents. **Child Study Journal, 19**(1), 41-50.

Elementary school children described in writing what their grandparents meant to them. Girls more frequently mentioned love than boys.

* Raymond, C.L., Benbow, C.P., & Persson, C. (1986). Gender differences in mathematics: a function of parental support and student sex typing. **Developmental Psychology.** (Cited as entry 368.)

243. Seitz, V., et al. (1985). Effects of family support intervention: a ten-year follow-up. **Child Development**, **56**(2), 376-91.

The delivery to impoverished mothers of medical and social services, including day care for their children, had effects that were evident 10 years later. These effects included higher socioeconomic status and educational attainment and smaller families for the mothers, and better school attendance and fewer academic problems for their children. Sex differences are discussed.

244. Slater, E.J., et al. (1983). The effects of family disruption on adolescent males and females. **Adolescence**, **18**(72), 931-42.

Examines the effects of separation and divorce on adolescents' self-image, anxiety, locus of control, and perception of their family. Results indicate males from disrupted homes had better self-concepts and seven better perceptions of their family environment than those from intact homes. The opposite results were found among females.

245. Smith, T.E. (1984). School grades and responsibility for younger siblings: an empirical study of the "teaching function". **American Sociological Review**, **49**(2), 248-60.

A study based on the confluence model of family effects upon intellectual growth found a negative relationship between grades and the number of older siblings for whites but not for blacks and a negative relationship between the grades of blacks and responsibility for younger siblings. Sex differences are discussed.

246. Stern, M., et al. (1984). Father absence and adolescent

"problem behaviors": alcohol consumption, drug use and sexual activity. **Adolescence, 19**(74), 301-12.

Reports results of a survey of adolescents to examine the relationship between father absence and adolescent drug use and sexual activity. Father absence was related to behavior problems, especially for boys.

* Tauber, M.A. (1979). Parental socialization techniques and sex differences in children's play. **Child Development.** (Cited as entry 794.)

247. Usui, W.M., et al. (1981). Determinants of parental expectations for children's education and occupation. **Sociology and Social Research, 65**(4), 415-23.

Reports data analyses suggesting that family social status, race, sex, and child's ability influence parents' expectations of educational and occupational attainment for the child.

248. Wilson, J., et al. (1983). The effects of age, occupation, race and education on parent communication with the school. **Education, 103**(4), 402-04.

Teachers and parents of third- and fourth-grade students at four randomly selected Gary, Indiana schools participated in a study of effects of age, occupation, race, and education on parent-school communication. Parents who were housewives, high school graduates, and/or 20- to 30-years-old were particularly satisfied with teacher-parent interaction. Sex differences are discussed.

* Wright, P.H., & Keple, T.W. (1981). Friends and parents of a sample of high school juniors: an exploratory study of relationship intensity and interpersonal rewards. **Journal of Marriage and the Family.** (Cited as entry 488.)

249. Zakariya, S.B. (1982). Another look at the children of divorce: summary report of the Study of School Needs of One-Parent Children. **Principal, 62**(1), 34-37.

A reanalysis of 1979-80 data collected on children of one-parent families (from a study published in this magazine in September 1980) reveals family income and student sex had a greater effect on achievement than did number of parents in the home.

Help Seeking | Helping Behavior

250. Brehm, S.S., et al. (1984). The effects of empathic instructions on donating behavior: sex differences in young children. **Sex Roles: A Journal of Research**, **10**(5-6), 405-16.

Results show that empathic instructions (in which children were told to imagine themselves in the target person's place) enhanced donating behavior for male first graders but had no effect on females.

251. Brooks, M.L. (1981). Evaluation of emotionally disturbed primary school age boys and girls by mental health workers and educators. **Journal for Special Educators, 17**(4), 344-51.

Reports results of a study in which mental health workers and educators rated the degree of emotional disturbance and needed treatment of four modified case histories. Sex differences are discussed.

252. Nelson-LeGall, S., DeCooke, P.A. (1987). Same-sex and cross-sex help exchanges in the classroom. **Journal of Educational Psychology**, **79**(1), 67-71.

Examines same-sex and cross-sex help exchanges in reading and math classes among third and fifth-grade students. Students sought help more frequently from same sex. Girls, more than boys, reported liking their boy helpers as much as their same-sex helpers.

253. Nelson-LeGall, S., Glor-Sheib, S. (1985). Help seeking in elementary classrooms: an observational study. **Contemporary Educational Psychology, 10**(1), 58-71.

Explores elementary students use of help seeking as a means of problem solving in the classroom. In-depth naturalistic observations were made of high-, average-, and low-ability students in first, third, and fifth grade reading and math classes. Implications for children's achievement, learning, and social adjustment are discussed. Sex differences are discussed.

254. Northman, J.E. (1985). The emergence of an appreciation for help during childhood and adolescence. **Adolescence, 20**(80), 775-81.

Investigates developmental changes in the perceived usefulness of help from the perspective of the person receiving the help. Results indicate an increase in the perceived usefulness of help across the school-age years. Girls consistently perceived help as being more useful than boys, and girls were generally rated as the most effective helpers.

* Vernon, S.W., & Roberts, R.E. (1985). A comparison of Anglos and Mexican-Americans on selected measures of social support. **Hispanic Journal of Behavioral Sciences.** (Cited as entry 170.)

Language | Reading | Literature

255. Ackerman, P.T., et al. (1983). Sex and group differences in reading and attention disordered children with and without hyperkinesis. **Journal of Learning Disabilities, 16**(7), 407-15

Reports results of a study of four groups of 7- to 10-year-old girls, either (1) hyperactive, (2) reading disabled, (3) hyperactive and reading disabled, or (4) solely attention disordered. Subjects were contrasted with male counterparts on measures of intelligence, achievement, personality, and cognitive style. Significant sex differences across groups on six measures are reported.

256. Badian, N.A. (1984). Reading disability in an epidemiological context: incidence and environmental correlates. **Journal of Learning Disabilities, 17**(3), 129-36.

Reports that among four-year groups of children in a school system 4 percent had a reading disability and 2.7 percent were "slow learners." Reading disabled boys tended to be later born in their families. Lower reading scores were associated with hot birth month temperatures for all socioeconomic groups.

257. Baldwin, R.S., et al. (1985). Effects of topic interest and prior knowledge on reading comprehension. **Reading Research Quarterly**, **20**(4), 497-504.

Examines effects of prior knowledge and topic interest on reading comprehension of seventh- and eighth-grade students. Results suggest that both prior knowledge and topic interest were autonomous factors in reading comprehension. Sex differences are discussed.

258. Bank, B.J., et al. (1980). Sex roles, classroom instruction, and reading achievement. **Journal of Educational Psychology, 72**(2), 119-32.

Hypotheses about sex differences in reading achievement, including ones based on physical maturation, female teacher bias, teacher discrimination, feminization of reading, differential response to pupil behaviors, and sex-relevant teaching styles, are considered. Evidence for and against each is presented; implications are suggested.

259. Benbow, C.P., & Stanley, J.C. (1982). Intellectually talented boys and girls: educational profiles. **Gifted Child Quarterly, 26**(2), 82-88.

Scores on the Math and Verbal Scholastic Aptitude Test (SAT) of 873 mathematically talented students (eighth grade and under) reveal that boys and girls performed similarly on the verbal SAT but that boys had a significantly higher mean score on the math SAT.

260. Beyard-Tyler, K.C., & Sullivan, H.J. (1980). Adolescent reading preferences for type of theme and sex of character. **Reading Research Quarterly, 16**(1), 104-20.

Details two studies that investigated adolescents' preferences for type of theme and sex of character in contemporary realistic fiction. Findings show (1) subjects show preference for themes in which the central problem is resolved successfully, and (2) boys prefer to read about males while girls prefer to read about females.

261. Bodart, J. (1986). Booktalks do work: the effects of book-talking on attitude and circulation. **Illinois Libraries, 68**(6), 378-81.

Examines effectiveness of booktalks for high school students by measuring their attitudes toward reading and book circulation. A reading attitude survey used as a pretest and posttest showed no significant differences overall, although specific teachers affected their students' attitudes toward reading. Circulation showed a dramatic increase. Sex differences are reported.

262. Burkhalter, B.B., & Wright, J.P. (1984). Handwriting performance with and without transparent overlays. **Journal of Experimental Education, 52**(3), 132-35.

Reports results of comparing the handwriting achievement of children using transparent overlays for self-assessment and children not using the overlays. No significant differences between the groups were found. Girls' achievement was higher when legibility, letter formation, and spacing were considered.

263. Buttery, T.J., & Reitzammer, A.F. (1987). Creative writing: a study of selected story stimuli on second grade children. **Reading Improvement, 24**(4), 262-66.

Analyzes the creative writing of second-grade children in a suburban elementary school, comparing boys' and girls' creative writings when the composition was elicited from realistic fiction, fantasy, and fantasy in conjunction with stuffed animals and wind-up toys. Also examines combined creativity of boys' and girls' compositions and the three types of story stimuli.

264. Cahn, L.D. (1988). Sex and grade differences and learning rate in an intensive summer reading clinic. **Psychology in the Schools, 25**(1), 84-91.

Examines patterns of variance for sex and grade level using the Nelson Reading Test, the Gates-MacGintie Reading Test, and the Spache Diagnostic Reading Scales for first to eighth grade students referred for possible reading disabilities. Females outscore males significantly on all measures.

265. Canning, P.M., et al. (1980). Sex differences in the perceptual, visual-motor, linguistic and concept-formation abilities of retarded readers. **Journal of Learning Disabilities, 13**(10), 563-67.

Male and female retarded readers at two age levels (6.5 to 8.5 years and 10.5 to 12.5 years) did not differ significantly on a number of perceptual, visual-motor, linguistic, and concept formation abilities.

266. Connor, U. (1983). Predictors of second-language reading performance. **Journal of Multilingual and Multicultural Development, 4**(4), 271-88.

Reports results of a study of limited-English-speaking Vietnamese children (K-12) showing that the best predictors of reading performance were grade, Vietnamese language background, amount of English spoken at home, higher level paternal occupation, and ESL class participation. Gender, siblings, television viewing, library visits, and other parent characteristics were not shown to be significant.

267. Crittenden, M.R., et al. (1984). Developing effective study skills and self-confidence in academically able young adolescents. **Gifted Child Quarterly, 28**(1), 25-30.

Reports results of short course in study skills and written language skills resulting in improved self-concept, written language, and study skills for gifted underachievers. Gender and age-grade differences are noted along with implications for gifted education.

268. Dappen, L., & Reynolds, C.R. (1981). Factorial validity of the 1976 edition of the Metropolitan Readiness Test for males and females. **Psychology in the Schools, 18**(4), 413-16.

The 1976 Metropolitan Readiness Test was factor analyzed from responses of beginning first graders. Results show a single general readiness factor, consistent with prior research, best described the battery of eight subtests. This factor is invariant across sex when separate analyses for males and females are compared.

269. Davis, A.J. (1984). Sex-differentiated behaviors in non-sexist picture books. **Sex Roles: A Journal of Research, 11**(1-2), 1-16.

Compares behavior of male and female characters in nonsexist picture books with those in conventional picture books, finding several differences but little sex-typing in the conventional books. Female characters in nonsexist books were more nurturing and less aggressive than males in both types of book.

270. Day, K.C., et al. (1981). The development of orthographic linguistic awareness in kindergarten children and the relationship of this awareness to later reading achievement. **Reading Psychology, 2**(2), 76-87.

Reports results of a study in which orthographic linguistic awareness measured at the beginning of kindergarten was highly correlated with reading achievement measured at the end of first grade. Relationships were shown to be consistently higher for girls than for boys.

271. Dougherty, W.H., & Engel, R.E. (1987). An 80's look for sex equality in Caldecott winners and honor books. **Reading Teacher, 40**(4), 394-98.

Analyzes Caldecott winners and honor books of the 1980's, comparing the findings to those of earlier studies to discover if the depiction of sex roles and characteristics has changed. Concludes that the newer books reflect a shift toward sex equality and provide some changing sex characteristics and roles--but not enough.

* Finn, J.D. (1980). Sex differences in educational outcomes: a cross-national study. **Sex Roles: A Journal of Research.** (Cited as entry 9.)

272. Graves, M.F., et al. (1980). Word frequency as a predictor of students' reading vocabularies. **Journal of Reading Behavior, 12**(2), 117-27.

Reports results of a study of word frequency as a predictor of high school students' reading vocabularies and the effects of grade, ability, and sex on word knowledge.

273. Graves, M.F., et al. (1987). The relationship between word frequency and reading vocabulary using six metrics of frequency. **Journal of Educational Research, 81**(2), 81-90.

Investigates the relationship between word frequency and reading vocabulary for elementary and secondary students. Particular attention is given to the lognormal model of word frequency distribution and the concept of family frequency. The effects of grade, ability, and gender are discussed.

* Greaney, V., & Neuman, S.B. (1983). Young people's views of the functions of reading: a cross-cultural perspective. **Reading Teacher.** (Cited as entry 158.)

274. Hadley, I.L. (1987). Understanding cohesion: some practical teaching implications. **Reading, 21**(2), 106-14.

Reports results of a study examining relationship between understanding of specific cohesive items and general reading comprehension ability. Sex differences are discussed.

275. Hahn, C.L. (1986). Are teachers prejudiced against students writing on non-traditional topics for their gender? **Journal of Social Studies Research**, **10**(1), 31-39.

Reports results of a study determining whether teachers' evaluations of student essays are influenced by sex role expectations. Contrary to similar research on non-teachers, pre-service and in-service teachers in this study evaluated elementary students' essays consistently, regardless of sex of the author.

276. Hale, R.L., & Potok, A.A. (1980). Sexual bias in the WISC-R. **Journal of Consulting and Clinical Psychology, 48**(6), 776.

Reports that while Verbal IQ of the Wechsler Intelligence Scale for Children predicts statistically distinct Wide Range Achievement Test Reading scores dependent on the sex of the child, differences are of little practical importance.

277. Hartley, J., & Trueman, M. (1985). A research strategy for text designers: the role of headings. **Instructional Science, 14**(2), 99-155.

Reports description of 17 experiments on effects of headings in written text, focuses on heading position, and form and nature of task (free recall, searching unfamiliar text, and retrieval from familiar text). Results indicate heading position had no effect but both heading forms aided recall, search, and text information retrieval. Sex differences are discussed.

278. Hogrebe, M.C., et al. (1985). Are there gender differences in reading achievement? An investigation using the high school and beyond data. **Journal of Educational Psychology, 77**(6), 716-24.

Reports findings of a study to investigate the relation of gender to reading achievement at the high school level. Findings suggest that by the time students reach high school, the magnitude of gender differences in reading achievement as assessed by the High School and Beyond survey is small.

279. Husak, W.S., & Magill, R.A. (1979). Correlations among perceptual-motor ability, self-concept and reading achievement in early elementary grades. **Perceptual and Motor Skills, 48**(2), 447-50.

Investigates correlations among measures of perceptual-motor abilities, self-concept, and reading achievement for elementary school students. Also examines whether perceptual-motor ability and self-concept score can predict reading achievement in the early elementary grades. Sex differences are discussed.

280. Johnson, C.S., & Greenbaum, G.R. (1980). Are boys disabled readers due to sex-role stereotyping? **Educational Leadership, 37**(6), 492-96.

A summary of research findings suggests cultural expectations account for the difference in reading achievement between boys and girls.

281. Johnson, D.M., et al. (1984). Protagonist preferences among juvenile and adolescent readers. **Journal of Educational Research, 77**(3), 147-50.

Examines the relationship between reader preference and protagonist characteristics, specifically sex and age of main characters.

282. Jones, M. (1983). Reading skills of third graders in terms of behavior and other variables. **Spand Reading Improvement, 20**(3), 181-86.

Reveals significant correlations between all subtests of a standardized reading test and the behavior scores for girls, higher socioeconomic background students, and non-black students. Significant correlations did not occur between the subtests and behavior scores for boys, lower socioeconomic background students, or blacks.

283. Jorm, A.F., et al. (1984). Phonological recoding skills and learning to read: a longitudinal study. **Applied Psycholinguistics, 5**(3), 201-07.

Reports data from a study testing whether phonological recoding is important during reading acquisition. Children who had no measurable phonological recoding skills were matched to children who had some skills in this domain and compared on reading performance at the end of grades one and two. Those with phonological recoding skills were significantly ahead. Sex differences are reported.

284. Klein, H.A. (1979). What effect does non-sexist content have on the reading of boys and girls? **Reading Improvement, 16**(2), 134-38.

Reports conclusions that both boys and girls benefitted from reading sex-appropriate content as opposed to content that was self-selected. Confirms that strong group feelings about reading exist outside a sex-typed pattern of interests.

* Klein, J.D., et al. (1987). The effects of age of viewer and gender of the narrator on children's visual attention and recall of story ideas. **Educational Communication and Technology Journal.** (Cited as entry 93.)

285. Lambert, J.C. (1985). Class discussion and one-to-one interaction: their effect on the decisions of fourth graders to write. **Journal of Educational Research, 78**(5), 315-18.

Investigates the effect of class discussion, one-to-one interaction, or no prewriting activity on the voluntary writing decisions of fourth graders. No differences were found for boys; however, the proportion of control group girls who chose to write was significantly higher than those in the class discussion group.

286. Lawson, A.E., & Shepherd, G.D. (1979). Syntactical complexity in written language and cognitive development at the formal level. **Science Education, 63**(1), 73-81.

Investigates the relationship between syntactical complexity of high school students' written language and their ability to reason formally. Format reasoning ability of high school students was measured by a 15-item group-administered demonstration test developed by Lawson. Sex differences are discussed.

* Leinhardt, G., et al. (1979). Learning what's taught: sex differences in instruction. **Journal of Educational Psychology.** (Cited as entry 566.)

287. McKenna, M.C. (1986). Reading interests of remedial secondary school students. **Journal of Reading, 29**(4), 346-51.

Investigates the reading interests of low ability junior and senior high readers of both sexes. Results indicate that readers of both sexes share some reading interests--among them topics dealing with the unusual.

288. Morrow, L.M., & Weinstein, C.S. (1986). Encouraging voluntary reading: the impact of a literature program on

children's use of library centers. **Reading Research Quarterly, 21**(3), 330-46.

Reports that while an intervention program increased children's library use, it did not affect their attitudes toward reading or their home reading habits. Sex differences are reported.

289. Murphy-Berman, V., & Jean, P.J. (1981). The factors affecting the gender connotations of language for the deaf child. **American Annals of the Deaf, 126**(1), 57-63.

Examines the adequacy of replacing generics with more gender neutral terms (e.g., "someone" for "people") for eight to eighteen year old hearing impaired students. Results show generally that neutral terms enabled students to limit masculine bias.

290. Nagle, R.J. (1979). The predictive validity of the Metropolitan Readiness Tests, 1976 Edition. **Educational and Psychological Measurement, 39**(4), 1043-45.

A sample of first-grade children was tested on the Metropolitan Readiness Tests, 1976 Edition (MRT), during the initial month of school and was retested eight months later on the Stanford Achievement Test. Results demonstrate substantial validity of the MRT for predicting first-grade achievement. Sex differences are discussed.

291. Nutter, N. (1982). The effects of "consciousness of correctness" on amount, fluency, and syntax of adolescents' speech. **Research in the Teaching of English, 16**(2), 149-70.

Investigates relative effects of directing adolescents' attention, either toward the "correctness" of their speech or toward the expression of their attitudes, on the amount, fluency, and syntactic structure of speech produced in a subsequent standardized interview. Sex differences are discussed.

292. Ollila, L., et al. (1989). Gender-related preferences for the choice of particular animals as writing topics in grade 1. **Journal of Research and Development in Education, 22**(2), 37-41.

Reports results of a study in which first grade children were asked to imagine they were animals and to write about their selections. Boys tended to identify themselves with animals characterized as strong, dangerous, or wild. Girls tended to link themselves with animals seen as weak, safe, or tame.

293. Olson, A., & Davies, A. (1989). The influence of gender differences on story retellings. **Reading, 23**(1), 32-38.

Investigates differences between female and male students' retellings of a story read silently. Findings show boys more productive than girls since the main character of the story was perceived to be male. Suggests students be allowed to self-select reading materials to maximize usefulness of previous knowledge.

294. Otteson, J.P., & Otteson, C.R. (1980). Effect of teacher's gaze on children's story recall. **Perceptual and Motor Skills, 50**(1), 35-42.

Reports results of two studies using a repeated-measures design to compare the story recall performances of primary-school children who were administered stories in the presence and absence of teacher's gaze. Analysis indicates a significant positive relationship between gaze and recall, especially among boys.

295. Parker, A., & Paradis, E. (1986). Attitude development toward reading in grades one through six. **Journal of Educational Research, 79**(5), 313-15.

Reports results of a study in which reading attitude inventory was administered to children in grades 1 through 6 to see if attitudes changed as students progressed through the grades. A difference was found between grades 4 and 5 which appeared to involve a more positive attitude toward non-classroom reading. Sex differences are reported.

296. Peck, K.L., & Hannafin, M. (1983). The effects of notetaking pretraining and the recording of notes on the retention of aural

instruction. **Journal of Educational Research, 77**(2), 100-07.

Reports that notetaking training affected sixth grade students' notetaking style but did not result in superior retention of aurally presented material. Also reports significant interactions between instruction in notetaking and the recording of notes, sex of student and notetaking, and notetaking and time.

297. Price, G.B., & Graves, R.L. (1980). Sex differences in syntax and usage in oral and written language. **Research in the Teaching of English, 14**(2), 147-53.

Reports that study of language usage of middle school students revealed no significant difference between the sexes on any measure of syntactic maturity. However, boys deviated from standard usage somewhat more frequently than girls. Boys produced more words in oral language while girls produced more words in written language.

298. Reeves, C., et al. (1989). Emergent literacy: an exploratory study of the effects of an expanded language experience approach. **International Journal of Early Childhood, 21**(1), 59-76.

Investigates effects of an expanded Language Experience Approach (LEA) on emergent literacy skills of kindergartners. Results indicate the expanded LEA is more effective than traditional LEA for development of listening comprehension skills in kindergartners. Sex differences are discussed.

299. Reynolds, C.R. (1979). The invariance of the factorial validity of the Metropolitan Readiness Tests for blacks, whites, males, and females. **Educational and Psychological Measurement, 39**(4), 1047-52.

Reports results of factor analysis of the six subtests comprising the Metropolitan Readiness Tests for white females, white males, black females, and black males. A single factor is reported as best describing the structure of the test for each group. The factor structure is essentially invariant with regard to race and sex variables.

300. Richmond, V.P., & Gorham, J. (1988). Language patterns and gender role orientation among students in grades 3-12. **Communication Education, 37**(2), 142-49.

Investigates current generic referent usage among public school children in grades 3-12. Reports an overall relationship between referent usage and gender role orientation, with more use of nontraditional referents among students who projected themselves in nontraditional occupational roles.

301. Riding, R.J., & Pugh, J.C. (1981). Visual performance and reading in seven and eleven year old children. **Journal of Research in Reading, 4**(1), 17-28.

Reports results of a test of visual performance designed to measure children's dark interval threshold. Differences are reported between boys and girls.

302. Riding, R.J., & Smith, E.M. (1984). Reading accuracy as a function of teaching strategy, personality and word complexity in seven-year-old children. **Educational Studies, 10**(3), 263-72.

Reports results of a study showing that the reading accuracy of seven-year-old children was significantly better with the installment rather than the whole method of oral reading. In addition, word complexity, extroversion, and sex interacted on reading accuracy.

303. Riding, R.J., & Vincent, D.J.T. (1980). Listening comprehension: the effects of sex, age, passage structure and speech rate. **Educational Review, 32**(3), 259-66.

Reports of a study in which four age groups, between 7 and 15, listened to a prose passage delivered at a slow or fast speech rate and structured to join or separate related pieces of information. A recall test followed immediately. Performance is correlated to subjects' age and sex.

304. Rie, E.D., & Rie, H.E. (1979). Reading deficits and intellectual

patterns among children with neurocognitive dysfunctions. **Intelligence, 3**(4), 383-89.

Reports results of calculating reading deficits among elementary-aged learning disabled children with suspected neurocognitive dysfunctions. Findings indicate pattern of high verbal-low performance IQs is associated with least deficiency in reading; this association is evident as early as second grade. Sex differences are discussed.

305. Romatowski, J.A., & Trepanier-Street, M.L. (1987). Gender perceptions: an analysis of children's creative writing. **Contemporary Education, 59**(1), 17-19.

Analyzes creative writing of first- through sixth-graders, showing strong male predominance in stories and other evidence of stereotypic thinking and gender bias.

306. Roscoe, B., et al. (1985). Written forms of self-expression utilized by adolescents. **Adolescence, 20**(80), 841-44.

Examines the writing forms used as a means of self-expression by high school students. Results indicate the majority of participants used at least one writing mode. Females and those who were juniors in high school reported more frequent use of these than did males and seniors.

307. Scott, K.P., & Feldman-Summers, S. (1979). Children's reactions to textbook stories in which females are portrayed in traditionally male roles. **Journal of Educational Psychology, 71**(3), 396-402.

Assesses effects of portraying female main characters in traditionally male roles on male and female children's sex role perceptions and story evaluations. Exposure to nontraditional female characters increased children's perceptions of number of girls who could engage in activities presented in the stories only.

308. Shapiro, J.E. (1980) Primary children's attitudes toward reading

in male and female teachers' classrooms: an exploratory study. **Journal of Reading Behavior, 12**(3), 255-57.

Reports results of a study indicating male primary school teachers may have some positive effect on children's attitudes toward reading. Sex differences are discussed.

309. Simpson, R.G., et al. (1984). The relationship between performance on the Wepman Auditory Discrimination Test and reading achievement among adolescents. **Educational and Psychological Measurement, 44**(2), 353-58.

Investigates the relationship between auditory discrimination, as measured by the Wepman Auditory Discrimination Test, and reading achievement, as measured by the Woodcock Reading Mastery Tests. After controlling for intelligence, there was little more than a random relationship between auditory discrimination and reading achievement. Sex differences are discussed.

310. Starko, A.J. (1989). Problem finding in creative writing: an exploratory study. **Journal for the Education of the Gifted, 12**(3), 172-86.

Reports results of a study investigating techniques used to generate and select topics for creative writing by professional writers, high school students with a specific interest in writing, high school students in above-average English classes, and students in average English classes. Sex differences are discussed.

311. Stevens, K.C. (1981). Reading interests among fifth and sixth grade children. **Reading Horizons, 21**(2), 147-50.

Reports results of an interest survey given to children in four fifth and sixth grade classrooms to determine if the sex differences in interest reported by earlier researchers were still in effect. Findings show differences in reading material preferences between males and females still existing.

312. Stewart, J.M., & Spells, V.R. (1983). Learning disabilities with

communicative disorders as related handicaps: a two-year study. **Journal of Communication Disorders, 16**(5), 345-55.

Summarizes a demographic profile of 494 learning disabled students who also exhibited related communication disorders and the impact of this population on speech-language and hearing services. Racial and sexual factors are also examined.

313. Stoefen-Fisher, J.M. (1985). Reading interests of hearing and hearing-impaired children. **American Annals of the Deaf, 130**(4), 291-96.

Reports results of a reading interest inventory administered to hearing-impaired students and hearing students between the ages of 9 and 12. Hearing-impaired students had a broader base of interests than their hearing peers. Sex was a significant factor affecting hearing students' cluster choices but was not pervasive for the hearing-impaired students.

314. Stoner, S.B., & Spencer, W. (1983). Sex differences in expressive vocabulary of Head Start children. **Boyd Perceptual and Motor Skills, 56**(3), 1008.

Reports results of a study in which the Expressive One-Word Picture Vocabulary Test was administered to males and females from 45 to 80 months of age to determine sex differences in the expressive vocabulary of Head Start children. Data indicates no significant sex differences.

315. Swanson, B.B. (1982). The relationship of first graders' reading attitude to sex and social class. **Reading World, 22**(1), 41-47.

Findings of this study suggest that sex and socioeconomic status of first grade students have little influence on their reading attitudes.

316. Thompson, G.B. (1987). Three studies of predicted gender differences in processes of word reading. **Journal of**

Educational Research, 80(4), 212-19.

Reports results of three studies conducted to examine individual differences among 6- and 7-year-olds in the use of alternative cognitive processes for word reading. The expectation that boys tend to rely more than girls, of the same reading level, on access to phonological segments of words is suggested.

317. Tibbetts, S. (1979). Sex-role stereotyping in children's reading material: update. **Journal of the NAWDAC, 42**(2), 3-9.

Reviews recently published children's reading material, finding evidence of book companies' efforts to eliminate sex-role stereotyping in publications.

318. Toifel, R.C., & Davis, W.D. (1983). Investigating library study skills of children in the public schools. **Journal of Academic Librarianship, 9**(4), 211-15.

Investigates library study skills of randomly selected students in grades 5, 8, and 11 using scores from Gullette-Hatfield Test of Library Skills to represent gender, grade level, and a socio-economic status of family. Review of literature, hypotheses, methodology (subjects, instruments, procedures, design), and results are included.

319. Tollefson, N., et al. (1985). Predicting reading achievement for kindergarten boys and girls. **Psychology in the School, 22**(1), 34-39.

Assesses the validity of the Kindergarten Teacher Rating Scale (KTRS) in predicting reading achievement for male and female students. Results indicate that the KTRS was a significant predictor of reading achievement for both boys and girls. Differential predictive validity for boys and girls was not found.

320. Trepanier-Street, M.L., & Romatowski, J.A. (1986). Sex and age differences in children's creative writing. **Journal of Humanistic Education and Development, 25**(1), 18-27.

Stories written by school-age children were examined for sex and age differences in the assignment of emotions and prosocial and aggressive behaviors to the story characters.

* Varner, I.I., & Grogg, P.M. (1988). Microcomputers and the writing process. **Journal of Business Communication.** (Cited as entry 148.)

321. Voeller, K.S., & Armus, J. (1986). A comparison of reading strategies in genetic dyslexics and children with right and left brain deficits. **Annals of Dyslexia, 36**, 270-86.

Reports results of a study comparing the reading levels of children (ages 7-16) with either genetic dyslexia, right-hemisphere lesions/dysfunction, or left-hemisphere lesions/dysfunction. Sex differences are reported.

322. Walden, J., Jr. (1979). A comparison of the PIAT and WRAT: a closer look. **Psychology in the Schools, 16**(3), 342-46.

Compares performances on Peabody Individual Achievement Test (PIAT) Math, Spelling, and Reading subtests with Wide Range Achievement Test (WRAT) Arithmetic, Spelling, and Reading subtests for a sample of fourth-graders. Nearly all PIAT-WRAT intercorrelations are shown as positive and significant, and highest for similarly labeled subtests. Sex differences are discussed.

323. Wendelin, K.H. (1980). Taking stock of children's preferences in humorous literature. **Reading Psychology, 2**(1), 34-42.

Discusses children's attitudes toward humorous stories, variables regarding children's sense of humor, and results of a study examining the relationship between children's grade level and sex and their preference for and perception of select elements of humor.

324. Wentzel, K.R. (1989). Gender differences in math and English achievement: a longitudinal study. **Sex Roles: A Journal of Research, 18**(11-12), 691-699.

Investigates gender-related developmental trends in math and English achievement as measured by classroom grades and standardized test scores of subjects followed from 6th through 12th grade. Results confirm hypotheses (1) that female classroom grades would remain stable over time, but that achievement test scores in the 2 subject areas would decline, and (2) that for males both assessment contexts would remain stable.

325. Western, L.E. (1979). Magazine preferences of fourth- and sixth-grade children. **Elementary School Journal, 79**(5), 284-91.

Reports results of a study of children in two metropolitan school districts in southeastern Wisconsin inquiring about children's preferences in magazines. Sex differences are discussed.

326. Whyte, J., & Harland, R. (1984). Sex differences in visual encoding skills: reading symbols. **Reading Psychology, 5**(1-2), 31-38.

Reports results of a study concluding that there may be differential effectiveness of method of reading instruction according to sex. Reports that females found letter training simpler than word training and that males found the reverse.

327. Williams, A.J., et al. (1987). Sex role socialization in picture books: an update. **Social Science Quarterly, 68**(1), 148-56.

Updates early research on how females are depicted in children's picture books. While the ratio of females to males is now closer to parity, storybook characters continue to portray traditional views of females.

328. Wolfson, B.J., et al. (1984). Revisiting what children say their reading interests are. **Reading World, 24**(2), 4-10.

Reports results of a study that reveal (1) some sex differences in children's reading preferences; (2) minority and nonminority preferences (but with more similarities than differences); (3) children's reading interests have changed little in two decades.

329. Wright, C.D., & Wright, J.P. (1980). Handwriting: the effectiveness of copying from moving versus still models. **Journal of Educational Research, 74**(2), 95-98.

Reports results of a study in which pupils used a moving model of letter formation in the form of a flipbook. Findings show lower skill improvement for students using a still model. Sex differences are discussed.

* Yore, L.D., et al. (1988). Exploration of the predictive and concurrent validity of a global measure of cognitive development for grade 1 reading, mathematics, and writing achievement. **Journal of Research and Development in Education.** (Cited as entry 123.)

330. Yore, L.D., & Ollila, L. (1985). Cognitive development, sex, and abstractness in grade one word recognition. **Journal of Educational Research, 78**(4), 242-47.

Reports results of a study on the effects of global cognitive development, sex, and word abstractness on young readers' word recognition. ANOVA results indicate that nouns were recognized more frequently than non-nouns; children with high cognitive development recognized more words than children with lower cognitive development; and females recognized more words than males.

Mathematics

331. Becker, J.R. (1981). Differential treatment of females and males in mathematics classes. **Journal for Research in Mathematics Education, 12**(1), 40-53.

Reports results of a study in which ten high school geometry teachers were observed to determine if there was differential treatment of male and female students. A trend of higher quantity and quality contacts with male students is reported.

332. Benbow, C.P., & Stanley, J.C. (1980). Sex differences in mathematical ability: fact or artifact? **Science, 210**(4475), 1262-64.

Reports results that show substantial sex differences in mathematical reasoning ability in favor of males. Data was collected in an investigation of intellectually gifted junior high school pupils who took the Scholastic Aptitude Test.

333. Benbow, C.P., & Stanley, J.C. (1983). Sex differences in mathematical reasoning ability: more facts. **Science, 222**(4627), 1029-031.

Reports results of a study indicating that seventh-grade students taking Scholastic Aptitude Test show large sex difference in mathematical reasoning ability. Among students scoring greater than 700, boys outnumbered girls 13 to 1. Hypothesized factors thought to influence the difference (such as course taking, attitudes) are not supported by data obtained.

334. Caldwell, J.H., & Goldin, G.A. (1979). Variables affecting word problem difficulty in elementary school mathematics. **Journal for Research in Mathematics Education, 10**(5), 323-36.

Compares relative difficulty of four types of word problems. Other variables considered are grade level, sex, order of testing, and performance on a computational skills test.

335. Callahan, L.G., & Clements D.H. (1984). Sex differences in rote-counting ability on entry to first grade: some observations. **Journal for Research in Mathematics Education, 15**(5), 378-82.

Data on sex differences in rote-counting ability for first-grade children are presented. Indicates how different data-gathering methods and different statistical treatments of the data can yield differing results.

336. Carpenter, T.P., et al. (1984). Achievement in mathematics: results from the National Assessment. **Elementary School Journal, 84**(5), 485-95.

Reports conclusions about the performance of 9-, 13-, and 17-year-old students on mathematics exercises in the 1973, 1978, and 1982 National Assessment of Educational Progress. Sex differences are reported.

337. Carpenter, T.P., et al. (1983). Results of the third NAEP Mathematics Assessment: secondary school. **Mathematics Teacher, 76**(9), 652-59.

Results from the third national mathematics assessment indicate that (1) the decline in performance of 17 year olds between 1973 and 1978 leveled out between 1978 and 1982, and (2) the performance of 13 year olds improved significantly between 1978 and 1982. However, most gains were on lower-order skills. Sex differences are discussed.

338. Cramer, R.H. (1989). Attitudes of gifted boys and girls towards math: a qualitative study. **Roeper Review, 11**(3), 128-31.

Reports results of a study of sex differences and stereotypes in gifted fourth grade students' attitudes toward mathematics. Harmful stereotypical thinking regarding females and mathematics is reported.

339. Dunton, K.J., McDevitt, T.M., & Hess, R.D. (1988). Origins of mothers' attributions about their daughters' and sons' performance in mathematics in sixth grade. **Merrill-Palmer Quarterly, 34**(1), 47-70.

Examines effect of children's gender on tendencies of mothers to use specific antecedents in ascribing causal explanations for their children's 6th-grade mathematics performance. Path analyses reveal that for both mothers of boys and mothers of girls, maternal perceptions of child performance show association with the attributions. For mothers of girls, only internal psychological sources, the mothers' effective relationships with their daughters, and the mothers' attributions about their own performance, show association with attribution of lack of ability in relative failure situations.

340. Duval, C.M. (1980). Differential teacher grading behavior toward female students of mathematics. **Journal for Research in Mathematics Education, 11**(3), 202-13.

Attempts to determine if teachers discriminate against female learners of mathematics. More than 1000 secondary mathematics teachers were asked to grade four geometry proofs. Student sex and ability were the independent variables. Analysis yielded no significant F ratios for either of the main effects or their interaction.

341. Eccles, J.S., & Jacobs, J.E. (1986). Social forces shape math attitudes and performance. **Signs, 11**(2), 367-80.

Challenges Benbow and Stanley's claim that boys are naturally better than girls at mathematics. Presents data counter to this conclusion and assesses the impact of the media's coverage of the Benbow and Stanley report on parents' attitudes. Concludes that math aptitude is strongly determined by parents' stereotypic beliefs.

342. Fennema, E., & Carpenter, T.P. (1981). Sex-related differences

in mathematics: results from national assessment. **Mathematics Teacher, 74**(7), 554-59.

Data from the second mathematics assessment of the National Assessment of Educational Progress show little difference between males and females in overall mathematics achievement at ages 9 and 13. However, at age 17, females are not achieving as well in mathematics as males.

343. Fennema, E., Tartre, L., & Lindsay, A. (1985). The use of spatial visualization in mathematics by girls and boys. **Journal for Research in Mathematics Education, 16**(3), 184-206.

Investigates how girls and boys who were discrepant in their spatial and verbal performance used spatial visualization skills in solving word problems and fraction problems. Findings show that low spatial visualization skill may be more debilitating to girls' mathematical problem solving than it is to boys.

344. Flexer, B.K. (1984). Predicting eighth-grade algebra achievement. **Journal for Research in Mathematics Education, 15**(5), 352-60.

Reports results of a study showing that algebra prognosis test scores and performance in seventh-grade mathematics best predicted algebra grades in grade eight. However, achievement on a standardized algebra test was best predicted by IQ, problem solving skills, and prognosis scores. No sex difference in achievement scores was found, but girls attained higher percentage grades.

345. Gallagher, S.A. (1989). Predictors of SAT mathematics scores of gifted male and gifted female adolescents. **Psychology of Women Quarterly, 13**(2), 191-203.

Examines predictor variables involved in the performance of male and female gifted high school juniors on the Scholastic Aptitude Test in mathematics (SAT-M). Concludes males demonstrate greater visual-spatial ability which plays a dominant role in SAT-M performance.

346. Hallinan, M.T., & Sorensen, A.B. (1987). Ability grouping and sex differences in mathematics achievement. **Sociology of Education, 60**(2), 63-72.

Argues that previous research overlooks the structural and organizational factors that affect sex differences in the mathematics achievement of school children. Examines, in particular, the effect of ability grouping. Concludes that sex is a factor in the assignment of students to ability groups and that males are more likely than females to be assigned to the high-ability group.

347. Hanna, G. (1989). Mathematics achievement of girls and boys in grade eight: results from twenty countries. **Educational Studies in Mathematics, 20**(2), 225-32.

Examines sex differences in mathematics achievement from a cross-cultural perspective using the data of the Second International Mathematics Study. Overall sex differences in geometry and measurement areas are reported. Data show differences among countries to be greater than sex differences.

348. Hanna, G., & Sonnenschein, J.L. (1985). Relative validity of the Orleans-Hanna Algebra Prognosis Test in the prediction of girls' and boys' grades in first-year algebra. **Educational and Psychological Measurement, 45**(2), 361-67.

Examines the relative predictive validity of girls' and boys' success in algebra. Scores of eighth-grade students on the Orleans-Hanna Algebra Prognosis Test were correlated with grades that students subsequently earned in first-year algebra. Algebra grades of girls proved to be the more predictable.

349. Hart, L.E. (1989). Classroom processes, sex of student, and confidence in learning mathematics. **Journal for Research in Mathematics Education, 20**(3), 242-60.

Reports comparisons of classroom interactions of seventh-grade girls and boys who differed in confidence in their ability to learn mathematics. Boys were involved in more public interactions with their teacher than girls. High-and low-confidence students showed little difference in their interactions with the teacher.

350. Heller, K.A., & Parsons, J.E. (1981). Sex differences in teachers' evaluative feedback and students' expectancies for success in mathematics. **Child Development, 52**(3), 1015-19.

Reports results of a study of two factors hypothesized to be related to sex differences in participation in mathematics courses: (1) teachers' evaluative feedback, (2) students' success expectations. No sex differences were found in patterns of teachers' evaluative feedback or students' success expectations on familiar mathematics tasks; however, girls had some lower success expectations than boys.

351. Herbert, W. (1982). Math ability: proof of sexual parity? **Science News, 121**(12), 198.

Examines a test of 1,366 high school students revealing no significant sex differences in the ability to perform geometrical proofs. Boys outscored girls on overall achievement in geometry, but the results are believed to reflect differential exposure to mathematics outside the classroom.

352. Isaacson, Z., & Freeman, H. (1980). Girls and mathematics--a response. **Mathematics Teaching, 90**, 24-26.

A critique of a research report which previously appeared in this journal. The research, concerned with the underachievement of girls in mathematics, is lauded for its intent but criticized on several counts, including equating ability and attainment and the choice of attitude factors used.

353. Jones, L.V. (1987). The influence on mathematics test scores, by ethnicity and sex, of prior achievement and high school mathematics courses. **Journal for Research in Mathematics Education, 18**(3), 180-86.

Reports that senior-year mathematics test scores are highly dependent on the number of mathematics courses taken at the level of

Algebra I or above. Sophomore students with similar levels of mathematics achievement may be expected to improve similarly regardless of race or sex by taking additional mathematics courses.

354. Karplus, R., et al. (1983). Early adolescents' proportional reasoning on 'rate' problems. **Educational Studies in Mathematics, 14**(3), 219-33.

Investigates qualitative features of proportional reasoning on dimensional intensive variables by sixth- and eighth-grade students. These features included types of comparison and types of strategies employed. Reports results based on the administration of four proportional problems, varying in numerical and referential content. Sex differences are discussed.

355. Kolata, G.B. (1980). Math and sex: are girls born with less ability? **Science, 210**(4475), 1234-35.

Examines the idea that females may be born with less mathematical ability than males. Data from Benbow and Stanley, as well as from the Education Commission of the States, are considered.

356. Leder, G. (1980). Bright girls, mathematics and fear of success. **Educational Studies in Mathematics, 11**(4), 411-22.

Two consistent areas of sex differences in mathematics are pointed out, along with the variety of reasons used to explain their causes. Two studies that examined students of both sexes who had revealed high mathematical abilities are discussed.

357. Leder, G. (1982). Mathematics achievement and fear of success. **Journal for Research in Mathematics Education, 13**(2), 124-35.

Reports results of a study (1) to delineate and describe sex differences in mathematics achievement and participation and (2) to investigate the usefulness of the fear of success construct in explaining the differences. Findings highlight the effects of environmental pressures on sex-related differences in mathematics performance and participation.

* Leinhardt, G., et al. (1979). Learning what's taught: sex differences in instruction. **Journal of Educational Psychology.** (Cited as entry 566.)

* Lindbeck, J.S. , & Dambrot, F. (1986). Measurement and reduction of math and computer anxiety. **School Science and Mathematics.** (Cited as entry 140.)

358. Marshall, S. (1983). Sex differences in mathematical errors: an analysis of distracter choices. **Journal for Research in Mathematics Education, 14**(5), 325-36.

Analyzes test data from 1976-79 on California children in grade six. Loglinear models were used to evaluate the consistency of response of each sex. A significant interaction between sex and choice of distracter occurred for a large majority of the items.

359. Midkiff, R.M., Burke, J.P., & Helmstadter, G.C. (1989). A causal model of mathematics performance in early adolescence: the role of sex. **Psychological Reports, 64**(1), 167-176.

Examines possible causal linkages for eighth graders among general scholastic aptitude, academic achievement in mathematics, self-concept of ability, and performance on a math examination using path analysis. Analysis shows sex differences in prediction of performance. For boys, performance could be predicted from scholastic aptitude and previous achievement in math. For girls, performance could be predicted only from previous achievement in math.

360. Miura, I.T., & Okamoto, Y. (1989). Comparisons of U.S. and Japanese first graders' cognitive representation of number and understanding of place value. **Journal of Educational Psychology, 81**(1), 109-14.

Reports assessment of the relationship between mathematics performance and fundamental linguistic variations in cognitive representation of numbers. Twenty-four first graders each from the United States and Japan were the subjects. Results indicate Japanese cognitive representation of number positively affects understanding of place value. No gender differences are reported.

361. Moore, E.G., & Smith, A.W. (1987). Sex and ethnic group differences in mathematics achievement: results from the National Longitudinal Study. **Journal for Research in Mathematics Education, 18**(1), 25-36.

Analyzes the mathematics achievement of males and females aged 15 to 22, who participated in the National Longitudinal Study of Youth Labor Force Behavior in 1980. Assessments are made for sex, education, and ethnic group effects. Generally, achievement of all groups increased the longer subjects remained in school.

362. Newman, R.S. (1984). Children's numerical skill and judgments of confidence in estimation. **Journal of Experimental Child Psychology, 37**(1), 107-23.

Investigates relationship of a basic numerical skill to perceptions of confidence on a task of quantitative estimation. Counting skill was related not only to accuracy in estimating but also to the appropriateness of subjects' confidence. Sex differences are reported.

363. Nibbelink, W.H., et al. (1986). Sex-role assignments in elementary school mathematics textbooks. **Arithmetic Teacher, 34**(2), 19-21.

Discusses suggestions for writing nonsexist textbooks. An analysis of problems in textbooks for grades 3-6 is presented, indicating that the texts are nonsexist but not antisexist.

364. Pedersen, K., et al. (1985). Attitudes and career interests of junior high school mathematics students: implications for the classroom. **Arithmetic Teacher, 32**(7), 45-49.

Reports results of a study defining negative attitudes toward, and negative behaviors in, mathematics on the part of junior high school females. Suggests that teachers alert to the pattern may facilitate attitude change. Four areas in which they can promote females' continuance in mathematics are defined.

365. Peterson, P.L., & Fennema, E. (1985). Effective teaching, student engagement in classroom activities, and sex-related differences in learning mathematics. **American Educational Journal, 22**(3), 309-35.

Reports results of a study of classroom activities related to mathematics achievement level of students in fourth-grade mathematics classes. Engagement in competitive mathematics activities, cooperative mathematics activities, social activities, and off-task behavior are reported as consistently and differentially related to girls' versus boys' low-level and high-level mathematics achievement.

366. Plake, B.S., et al. (1981). Sex differences in mathematics components of the Iowa Tests of Basic Skills. **Psychology of Women Quarterly, 5**(5), 780-84.

Investigates mathematics problem solving (MPS) and mathematics concepts (MC) subtests of the Iowa Tests of Basic Skills for content and psychometric item bias at grades three, six, and eight. Identifies items which favor either males or females. Found no skill classification, item content, or location trends.

* Pratt, D.L. (1985). Responsibility for student success/failure and observed verbal behavior among secondary science and mathematics teachers. **Journal of Research in Science Teaching.** (Cited as entry 574.)

367. Preece, M. (1979). Mathematics: the unpredictability of girls? **Mathematics Teaching, 87**, 27-29.

Investigates lack of females in mathematics related occupations, concluding that the problem lies partially in the attitudes of girls toward mathematics.

368. Raymond, C.L., Benbow, C.P., & Persson, C. (1986). Gender differences in mathematics: a function of parental support and student sex typing? **Developmental Psychology, 22**(6), 808-19.

Reports results of a study testing hypotheses with mathematically and verbally talented children that (1) mathematically related fields are sex typed as male domains and (2) parents give differential encouragement to sons and daughters in math. Results indicate that neither hypothesis related to current sex differences in mathematical reasoning ability for this group.

* Ridley, R., Novak, J., & Alberta, D. (1983). Sex-related differences in high school science and mathematics enrollments: do they give males a critical headstart toward science and math-related careers? **Journal of Educational Research.** (Cited as entry 618.)

369. Ross, S.M., & Anand, P.G. (1987). A computer-based strategy for personalizing verbal problems in teaching mathematics. **Educational Communication and Technology Journal, 35**(3), 151-62.

Describes investigation of the effectiveness of personalizing verbal math problems on division of fractions for fifth and sixth grades using microcomputer-generated lessons.

370. Rubenstein, R.N. (1985). Computational estimation and related mathematical skills. **Journal for Research in Mathematics Education, 16**(2), 106-19.

Reports results of a study of four types of computational estimation examined in relation to other mathematical skills and sex differences with eighth graders. Open-ended estimation was the most difficult, followed by estimation relative to a reference number and estimation within an order of magnitude.

371. Schofield, H.L. (1982). Sex, grade level, and the relationship between mathematics attitude and achievement in children.

Journal of Educational Research, 75(5), 280-84.

Reports results of a study examining data on mathematics attitudes and achievement of fourth through sixth grade students in relation to sex, grade level, type of achievement test, and time during the school year at which the measurements were taken.

372. Schwartz, H., & Papier, S. (1985). A head start in mathematics for girls in primary school: a pilot study. **Urban Education, 19**(4), 357-64.

The results of this study suggest that, as girls seem to be more receptive to learning at an earlier age, they should start in second or third grade with math enrichment over and above the regular math class.

373. Senk, S., & Usisejkin, Z. (1983). Geometry proof writing: a new view of sex differences in mathematics ability. **American Journal of Education, 91**(2), 187-201.

Results of a study of students in senior high school classes show that males and females had equal abilities in working geometry proofs. Results also held for select high-achieving subsamples.

374. Sherman, J. (1980). Mathematics, spatial visualization, and related factors: changes in girls and boys, grades 8-11. **Journal of Educational Psychology, 72**(4), 476-82.

Reports results of a study showing that although girls and boys were similar in cognitive skills and attitudes toward mathematics in grade 8, boys performed significantly better in mathematics by grade 11, even with mathematics background controlled. No sex-related difference in spatial visualization is shown.

375. Sherman, J. (1981). Girls' and boys' enrollments in theoretical math courses: a longitudinal study. **Psychology of Women Quarterly, 5**(5), 681-89.

Reports results of a study in which students were followed through high school to determine what factors in the ninth grade predicted their continuation in theoretical mathematics courses. Test results indicate for girls that standardized weights were highest for spatial visualization, vocabulary, usefulness and confidence; for boys, confidence, achievement, stereotyping math as a male domain, and motivation.

376. Sherman, J. (1980). Predicting mathematics grades of high school girls and boys: a further study. **Contemporary Educational Psychology, 5**(3), 249-55.

Reports results of a study of eighth-grade scores for 140 females and 115 males on three cognitive tests and the Fennema-Sherman Mathematics Attitudes Scales to predict mathematics grades 1-3 years later. In addition to mathematics achievement, significant relationships were confirmed for spatial visualization and confidence in learning mathematics.

377. Smead, V.S., & Chase, C.I. (1981). Student expectations as they relate to achievement in eighth grade mathematics. **Journal of Educational Research, 75**(2), 115-20.

Reports results of a study focusing on the effect of students' expectations for achievement in mathematics on actual achievement. Results indicate that student expectations relate to subsequent achievement and that no significant relationship between achievement and expectations based on sex role stereotypes exists.

378. Swafford, J.O. (1980). Sex differences in first-year algebra. **Journal for Research in Mathematics Education, 11**(5), 335-46.

Reports results of a study to determine whether female and male students with comparable mathematics backgrounds show comparable achievement patterns in algebra. Sex differences reported appear to have little relation to algebra.

379. Tsai, S., & Walberg, H.J. (1983). Mathematics achievement

and attitude productivity in junior high school. **Journal of Educational Research, 76**(5), 267-72.

Analyzes achievement test scores and ratings of 13-year-old students who participated in the 1977-78 National Assessment of Educational Progress. Reports that achievement was significantly associated with attitudes, sex, ethnicity, parents' education, verbal opportunities in the home, and frequency of mathematical practice.

* Wentzel, K.R. (1989). Gender differences in math and English achievement: a longitudinal study. **Sex Roles: A Journal of Research.** (Cited as entry 324.)

380. Wolleat, P.L., et al. (1980). Sex differences in high school students' causal attributions of performance in mathematics. **Journal for Research in Mathematics Education, 11**(5), 356-66.

Reports results of a study to (1) test causal attribution theory in the masculine-typed, content-specific task domain of mathematics, and (2) examine effects of level of mathematics achievement, sex, and the interaction level of achievement and sex on attribution patterns.

381. Wood, E.F. (1988). Math anxiety and elementary teachers: what does research tell us? **For the Learning of Mathematics, 8**(1), 8-13.

Presents a general overview of mathematics anxiety, its definition, and techniques to measure it. Includes a brief discussion of gender-related issues and an analysis of research on effects of mathematics anxiety on elementary teachers.

* Yore, L.D., et al. (1988). Explorations of the predictive and concurrent validity of a global measure of cognitive development for grade 1 reading, mathematics, and writing achievement. **Journal of Research and Development in Education.** (Cited as entry 123.)

Mental Health | Mental Well Being

382. Cantrell, V.L., & Prinz, R.J. (1985). Multiple perspectives of rejected, neglected, and accepted children: relation between sociometric status and behavioral characteristics. **Journal of Consulting and Clinical Psychology, 53**(6), 884-89.

Reports findings of a study of three groups of children (rejected, neglected, and accepted). Boys and girls were identified separately and were compared on peer behavioral attributions, teacher ratings, analogue assertiveness tasks, and self-evaluation. Rejected children were clearly distinguished from their same-sex neglected and accepted classmates and were described by teachers and peers as aggressive, disruptive, and inattentive.

383. Crowley, J.A. (1981). Worries of elementary school students. **Elementary School Guidance and Counseling, 16**(2), 98-102.

Reports results of a study in which students were questioned about their worries. Findings show the percentage of students who worry about grades is consistently high across grade levels. Over half the students worry about physical harm to themselves or loved ones. Suggests school counseling programs include relaxation training to help students cope with life stresses. Sex differences are discussed.

384. DeCasper, H.S., & Tittle, C.K. (1988). Rankings and ratings of values: counseling uses suggested by factoring two types

of scales for female and male eleventh grade students. **Educational and Psychological Measurement, 48**(2), 375-84.

Analyzes the factor structure of rankings and ratings of three sets of values, illustrating how counselors use them with adolescents. The analyses of gender-related differences suggest perspectives from which counselors may explore values students consider important in making decisions about occupations, marriage, and parenthood.

385. Finch, A.J., Jr., et al. (1985). Children's Depression Inventory. **Journal of Consulting and Clinical Psychology, 53**(3), 424-425.

Reports results of a study collecting normative data for the Children's Depression Inventory from public school children in grades 2 through 8. Reports significant sex and grade differences, but the absolute magnitude of these differences is small. Scores are shown as consistent with those previously reported.

386. Harris, J.D., et al. (1987). Referrals to school psychologists: a national survey. **Journal of School Psychology, 25**(4), 343-54.

Reports results of a national survey of elementary and secondary school psychologists regarding recent referrals. Findings show more boys than girls referred.

387. Moracco, J.C., & Camilleri, J. (1983). A study of fears in elementary school children. **Elementary School Guidance and Counseling, 18**(2), 82-87.

Investigates fears of third graders who completed a checklist of 25 items. Results show girls were generally more fearful than boys. Loss of parents was the principal source of fear. Fears of natural phenomena (tornados and storms) and of animals show greatest consistency.

* Newton, R.R. (1984). Maximum likelihood estimation of factor structures of anxiety measures: a multiple group comparison. **Educational and Psychological Measurement.** (Cited as entry 776.)

* Subotnik, R.F. (1988). The motivation to experiment: a study of gifted adolescents's attitudes toward scientific research. **Journal for the Education of the Gifted.** (Cited as entry 632.)

388. Worchel, F., et al. (1987). New perspectives on child and adolescent depression. **Journal of School Psychology, 25**(4), 411-14.

Reports results of administering Children's Depression Index to elementary and secondary school students. Females are reported showing more overall depression than males. Results suggest that females tend to internalize difficulties while males externalize them.

Miscellaneous

389. Aiello, J.R., et al. (1979). Physiological, social, and behavioral consequences of crowding on children and adolescents. **Child Development, 50**(1), 195-202.

Fourth-, eighth- and eleventh-grade children were exposed in groups of four to short-term conditions of high or moderate spatial density involving close physical proximity. Physiological responses were measured during this exposure; subjects engaged in a cooperation-competition activity and provided self-reports related to their participation. Sex differences are discussed.

390. Bardwell, R. (1984). The development and motivational function of expectations. **American Educational Research Journal, 21**(2), 461-72.

Reports results of a study in which fourth, sixth, and eighth grade students studied a word learning task and were tested on three consecutive days. Expectant statements were made by half the subjects, apparently contradicting previous research. The researcher explains the contradiction on the basis of task complexity. Expectations were found to be motivational. Sex differences are reported.

391. Bardwell, R. (1984). The learning of expectations and attributions. **Education and Treatment of Children, 7**(3), 237-45.

Reports results of a study assessing how children state expectations and make attributions. First-, fourth-, and sixth-graders were given either homogeneous or heterogeneous false feedback for four pages of perceptual judgment problems. Older children, girls and persons receiving homogenous feedback showed more accurate expectations than their counterparts.

392. Bart, W., et al. (1986). An ordering-analytic approach to the study of group differences in intelligence. **Educational and Psychological Measurement, 46**(4), 799-810.

An alternative way of studying group differences is proposed based on ordering analysis using item hierarchies as a basis of comparison between two groups. Subjects were sets of twins in elementary school. Results show that blacks and whites and males and females had similar item hierarchies for complex items.

393. Bearison, D.J., et al. (1986). Socio-cognitive conflict and cognitive growth in young children. **Merrill-Palmer Quarterly, 32**(1), 51-72.

Compares pairs of five- to seven-year-old children working collectively on spatial perceptive problems to control subjects working individually on the same problems. Although children working in dyads did not perform significantly better than children working alone, there were several critical features in the frequency and quality of social interaction promoting cognitive growth. Sex differences are discussed.

394. Bertelson, C.L. (1986). An assessment of decision-making styles/processes of consumer education students. **Delta Pi Epsilon Journal, 28**(3), 135-45.

Reports an assessment to determine the decision-making processes and styles used by consumer education students when confronted with a consumer credit problem. Findings reveal that gender plays a large role in the process and style used.

395. Brody, L.R. (1984). Sex and age variations in the quality and intensity of children's emotional attributions to hypothetical

situations. **Sex Roles: A Journal of Research, 11**(1-2), 51-59.

Stories were read to elementary age children who indicated how they would feel as the story protagonist. Boys attributed anger to themselves more frequently than did girls, who more often attributed sadness and fear to themselves. The intensity of both boys' and girls' emotional attributions decreased with age.

396. Burrus-Bammel, L.L., & Bammel, G. (1986). Gender test differences during an environmental camp. **Journal of Environmental Education, 17**(3), 8-11.

Reports results of a study to determine the effects of gender on test scores from participants of a week-long environmental camp. An analysis of three years of data of student attitudes, knowledge, expectations, and perceptions indicate that females were lower on knowledge pre-tests but made greater gains between knowledge tests.

397. Cohen, H.G. (1984). The effects of two teaching strategies utilizing manipulatives on the development of logical thought. **Journal of Research in Science Teaching, 21**(8), 769-78.

Investigates effects of two instructional strategies (related to student use of manipulative materials) on second-grade students' development of logical structures. Also examines the effects of sex on logical development. Results indicate that supplying manipulative materials alone is not adequate in promoting development of logical structures.

398. Cohen, M., et al. (1988). The Conners Teacher Rating Scale: effects of age, sex, and race with special education children. **Psychology in the Schools, 25**(2), 195-202.

Reports results of administering the Connors Teacher Rating Scale to special education and regular education students to examine effects of age, sex, and race on the Cohen and Hynd Factor Analysis. Findings support use of Cohen and Hynd Factor Analysis in providing clinically meaningful description of children's overall behavior patterns.

399. Cole, P.M. (1986). Children's spontaneous control of facial expression. **Child Development, 57**(6), 1309-21.

Examines spontaneous expressive control of negative emotion in two studies of children three- to nine-years-old, using an experimental "disappointing" situation. Sex differences are discussed.

400. Cox, D., & Waters, H.S. (1986). Sex differences in the use of organization strategies: a developmental analysis. **Journal of Experimental Child Psychology, 41**(1), 18-37.

Reports results of two experiments investigating sex differences in the use of organization strategies in free recall with categorizable and unrelated word lists across age in elementary school. Shows sex differences were pronounced across the ages tested and consistent with principles of strategy development. Males show a developmental lag in the use of organization strategies.

401. Davies, L. (1984). Political education, gender and the art of the possible. **Educational Review, 36**(2), 187-95.

Seeks to broaden definitions of politics and political education by focusing on gender. Suggests that political education should be a process of demystification, teaching that power can be challenged and problem-solving techniques can be used to inject skills and new styles of seeking political alternatives.

402. DeHaas, P.A. (1986). Attention styles and peer relationships of hyperactive and normal boys and girls. **Journal of Abnormal Child Psychology, 14**(3), 457-67.

Reports results of comparing attention styles and peer relationships of hyperactive and normal boys and girls in grades 3-5, using behavioral, cognitive, and sociometric measures. Hyperactive girls displayed more conduct problems than normal girls, but less than hyperactive boys.

403. De Pietro, R., & Allen, R.L. (1984). Adolescents' communication styles and learning about birth control.

Adolescence, 19(76), 827-37.

Reports results of a study identifying predictors of birth control knowledge resulting from interactant or noninteractant communication styles in adolescents who read a magazine on human sexuality. Data suggest that the interactant style was most beneficial for new learning. Gender and the presence of siblings in the home were important moderators. Sex differences are discussed.

404. Dorris, J.M. (1981). Androgyny and pedagogy: an analysis of interpersonal communication textbooks, 1975-79. **Communication Education, 30**(1), 33-43.

Analyzes the content of interpersonal textbooks regarding the use of gender identity in the area of interpersonal communication. Indicates texts favor androgyny, with masculinity mediated by femininity in terms of power, problem solving, and self-esteem, and femininity mediated by masculinity in terms of emotions and relationships.

405. Etaugh, C., et al. (1981). Children's causal attributions of female and male success and failure. **Journal of Psychology, 108**(2), 199-205.

Reports results of asking male and female preschoolers and third graders to explain the success and failure of girls and boys on feminine and masculine tasks by choosing among four causal factors: ability, effort, task difficulty, and luck.

406. Fabrizi, M.S., & Pollio, H.R. (1987). Naturalistic study of humorous activity in a third, seventh, and eleventh grade classroom. **Merrill-Palmer Quarterly, 33**(1), 107-28.

Considers four questions related to humorous activity: What events evoke laughter and smiling in classrooms and do these events change as children grow older? Are there differences in frequency and type of events produced and appreciated? How do teachers and peers react to humorous events? What are the other behavior patterns of children who produce humorous events? Sex differences are discussed.

407. Favero, J., et al. (1979). The concurrent validity and factor structure of seventeen structure-of-intellect measures reflecting behavioral content. **Educational and Psychological Measurement, 39**(4), 1019-34.

Reports results of a study of concurrent validity of measures of empathy and social sensitivity, conceptualized within the behavioral segment of Guilford's structure-of-intellect model. Sex differences are discussed.

408. Fleming, D.B. (1984). Students' and parents' views of **The Day After** and the place of nuclear war education in the schools. **Social Studies, 75**(1), 8-9.

Students and parents participating in this survey overwhelmingly supported the study of nuclear war in public schools. Twenty-three percent of the students indicated that **The Day After** strongly affected their views of nuclear war, 45 percent rated the program as fair, and 39 percent weren't sure how realistic it was. Sex differences are discussed.

409. Girondi, A.J. (1983). A discriminant analysis of attitudes related to the nuclear power controversy. **Journal of Environmental Education, 14**(4), 2-6.

Reports results of a study designed to (1) develop a test instrument for measuring selected attitudes toward nuclear power, (2) determine if attitudinal differences exist between selected groups of individuals, (3) describe group differences in attitude, and (4) classify group members as either anti- or pronuclear. Sex differences are discussed.

410. Hilgert, L.D., & Treloar, J.H. (1985). The relationship of the Hooper Visual Organization Test to sex, age, and intelligence of elementary school children. **Measurement and Evaluation in Counseling and Development, 17**(4), 203-06.

Reports results of administering the Hooper Visual Organization Test (VOT) to elementary students referred for psychometric evaluation. Results show no significant relationship between sex and VOT scores, but age and IQ are significant correlates.

411. Hotchkiss, L. (1986). Determinants of part-time work of high school seniors. **Journal of Industrial Teacher Education, 23**(4), 30-42.

Assesses effects on student part-time employment outcomes of personal characteristics (i.e., gender, race) and institutional characteristics (i.e., vocational high school, participation in cooperative education). Reports supply theory explains student employment outcomes better than demand theory.

412. Irvine, J.J. (1986). Teacher-student interactions: Effects of student race, sex, and grade level. **Journal of Educational Psychology, 78**(1), 14-21.

Reports results of a study of students' classroom initiation behaviors (and other factors) in relation to student race, sex, and grade level, using a modified Brophy-Good Observation System. Results indicate that male students initiate more positive and negative interactions with teachers than do female students.

413. Iso-Ahola, S.E., & Buttimer, K.J. (1982). On the measurement of work and leisure ethics and resultant intercorrelations. **Educational and Psychological Measurement, 42**(2), 429-35.

Reports results of a study moderately negatively correlating the work ethic and leisure ethic. Correlations between the ethics were influenced by gender differences and the types of items included in the instruments.

414. Jaffe, J., et al. (1985). Speed of color naming and intelligence: association in girls, dissociation in boys. **Journal of Communication Disorders, 18**(1), 63-66.

Reports results of a rapid naming test administered to prereaders (five-seven years old). Results show sex differences in degree of correlation between naming performance and a test of general intelligence. Results bear theoretically on the degree to which a learning disability can appear as an isolated deficit in the two sexes.

415. Jones, R.S. (1979). Changes in the political orientations of American youth: 1969-1975. **Youth and Society, 10**(4), 335-59.

Reports results of longitudinal data from a national sample of students ages 9, 13, and 17 used to study levels of political knowledge and participation among American youth. Changes in these levels from 1969 to 1975 are examined. Sex differences are discussed.

416. Kellert, S.R. (1985). Attitudes toward animals: age-related development among children. **Journal of Environmental Education, 16**(3), 29-39.

Reviews findings on children's knowledge, attitudes, and behaviors toward animals and natural habitats. Research results indicate existence of three stages in the development of children's perceptions of animals. Major differences in age, sex, ethnicity and urban/rural residence are also noted.

417. Knight, G.P., et al. (1985). Information processing and the development of cooperative, competitive, and individualistic social values. **Developmental Psychology, 21**(1), 37-45.

Assesses possibility that developmental difference in social values is associated with development of information processing capabilities. Three- to ten-year-old children completed an individualized regression assessment of social values, a central-incidental memory measure, and a free-recall word list task. Results indicate significant relation of age, sex, and memory to expression of social value.

418. Kourilsky, M., & Kehret-Ward, T. (1984). Kindergartners' attitudes toward distributive justice: experiential mediators. **Merrill-Palmer Quarterly, 30**(1), 49-64.

Explores aspects of experience that might establish a meaningful connection between work and entitlement in middle class kindergarten children from 21 California classrooms. Experimental groups received the Kinder-Economy Instructional System as treatment while the control group received regular social studies instruction. Sex differences are discussed.

419. Lambert, N.M. (1979). Contributions of school classification, sex, and ethnic status to adaptive behavior assessment. **Journal of School Psychology, 17**(1), 3-16.

Investigates contributions of school classification and sex and ethnic status to domain scores from the Public School Version of the AAMD Adaptive Behavior Scale. The results replicated earlier findings that domain scores are valid for differentiating among children of different adaptive behavior levels.

420. Littlefield, R.S., & Sellnow, T.L. (1987). The use of self-defense as a means for reducing stage-fright in beginning speakers. **Communication Education, 36**(1), 62-64.

Indicates that the "Sharing Feelings Speech" assignment (1) failed to support the hypothesis that self-disclosure reduces stage fright in public speaking situations more than other forms of public speaking, and (2) revealed no significant gender-based differences.

421. Marsh, H.W. (1989). Effects of attending single-sex and coeducational high schools on achievement, attitudes, behaviors, and sex differences. **Journal of Educational Psychology, 81**(1), 70-85.

Reports results of a comparison of the effects of single-sex versus coeducational arrangements for Catholic high school students representing single-sex boys', single-sex girls', and coeducational schools. Various outcomes during the sophomore-to-senior period are reported as nearly unaffected by school type. Findings contradict those of earlier national studies.

422. Martin, D.A., & Bender, D.S. (1985). "Trade-offs," field

dependence/independence, and sex-based economics comprehension differences. **Journal of Economic Education, 16**(1), 62-70.

Reports results showing that while field independent and field dependent sixth grade students had equal prior knowledge of economic concepts, field independent students learned more than field dependent students from "Trade-offs." Males were more field independent than females. Although males scored higher on the post-test, the difference is not statistically significant.

423. Matthews, M.H. (1986). Gender, graphicacy and geography. **Educational Review, 38**(3), 259-71.

Attempts to explain why geography seems to attract more boys than girls. Attention is given to how gender-related differences in spatial behavior around the home influence the development of mapping abilities. Recommends teachers be more aware of the influence of gender upon performance levels in geography.

424. Moore, J.W., et al. (1984). Racial prejudice, interracial contact, and personality variables. **Journal of Experimental Education, 52**(3), 168-73.

Reports the results of a study examining the relationship of childrens' racial prejudice to child's race, interracial contact, grade, sex, intelligence, locus of control, anxiety, and self-concept. Five facets of racial prejudice were examined: a total index of racial prejudice; dating and marriage; school relationships; social relationships; and racial interactions in restaurants.

425. Murphy-Berman, V., et al. (1986). Measuring children's attention span: a microcomputer assessment technique. **Journal of Educational Research, 80**(1), 23-28.

Reports results of measuring the attention span of boys and girls in kindergarten through the ninth grade by a microcomputer technique. Attentional ability increased only up through the fifth grade, and both the false alarm rate and the interstimulus interval scores were related to behavioral activity during test sessions. Sex differences are discussed.

426. Osborne, J.G., et al. (1984). Rapid community growth and the problems of elementary and secondary students. **Rural Sociology, 49**(4), 553-67.

Reports results of administering the Mooney Problem Checklist to a stratified random sample of elementary and secondary public school students in rural areas of Utah classed as rapidly growing. Effects related to rapid or slow community growth are specific to grade level and to problem domains of the check list. Sex differences are discussed.

427. Philliber, S.G., & Tatum, M.L. (1982). Sex education and the double standard in high school. **Adolescence, 17**(66), 273-83.

Reports results of a study surveying high school students and comparing those who had and had not taken sex education classes. Findings indicate gender identity exerts a significant impact on sexual attitudes and knowledge and age and grade achievement influence sexual behavior.

428. Pringle, G.F., et al. (1985). Speed of color naming and degree of familial sinistrality: correlation in girls, no correlation in boys. **Journal of Communication Disorders, 18**(1), 59-62.

Male and female right-handed children, aged five to seven, were assessed for the effect of familial sinistrality left-handedness on a rapid color naming task. Controlling for age and family size, a significant effect for degree of familial sinistrality is reported for girls but not for boys.

429. Richmond, P.G. (1980). Limited sex differences in spatial test scores with a preadolescent sample. **Child Development, 51**(2), 601-02.

Reports results of a study in which six pencil-and-paper spatial tests were administered to 232 boys and 237 girls with an average age of 10 years. Findings indicate sex differences in spatial ability may emerge before adolescence but are not necessarily generalized at that time.

430. Rierdan, J. (1980). Word associations of socially isolated adolescents. **Journal of Abnormal Psychology, 89**(1), 98-100.

Reports results of a study in which isolates emitted significantly greater proportion of idiosyncratic associates than did nonisolates. Findings also show isolates emitted idiosyncratic associates significantly earlier in a series of associations than nonisolates. Sex differences are discussed.

431. Rose, S.C., & Thornburg, K.R. (1984). Mastery motivation and need for approval in young children: effects of age, sex, and reinforcement condition. **Educational Research Quarterly, 9**(1), 34-42.

Investigates differences in the mastery motivation levels and approval needs of children, ages four and eight. Two groups of children each worked on puzzle tasks in one of two conditions: (1) verbal reinforcement or (2) nonreinforcement. Younger children needed more reinforcement than older children. Sex differences are discussed.

432. Ryckman, D.B. (1981). Sex differences in a sample of learning disabled children. **Learning Disability Quarterly, 4**(1), 48-52.

Examines sex differences between learning disabled (LD) girls and LD boys (all elementary school age) on psychological, academic, and cognitive style measures. LD girls were found to be verbally inferior, less capable of abstract thinking, more field dependent, and more impulsive than boys.

433. Ryckman, D.B., & Peckman, P.D. (1986). Gender differences on attribution patterns in academic areas for learning disabled students. **Learning Disabilities Research, 1**(2), 83-89.

Reports results of comparing causal attribution patterns of learning disabled (LD) boys and girls (grades 4-11) by using the Survey of Achievement Responsibility. Girls results show higher effort and luck attributions in academic success situations than do boys and higher ability attributions for academic failure situations.

434. Scott, K.P. (1984). Effects of an intervention on middle school pupils' decision making, achievement, and sex role flexibility. **Journal of Educational Research, 77**(6), 369-75.

Examines pupil decision making, achievement, and sex role flexibility in a year-long study of middle school students.

435. Shakeshaft, C. (1986). A gender at risk. **Phi Delta Kappan, 86**(7), 499-503.

Introduction to a special issue on women in education. Argues that evidence shows that neither equal treatment nor equality of outcome exists in most schools.

436. Sidelnick, D.J. (1989). Effects of ability, grade, and gender on three measures of citizenship with high school students. **Social Studies, 80**(3), 92-97.

Investigates differences in political attitudes among high school students of different ability and grade levels. Results show low ability subjects are more dogmatic. Sex differences are discussed.

437. Sieber, J.E. (1979). Confidence estimates on the correctness of constructed and multiple-choice responses. **Contemporary Educational Psychology, 4**(3), 272-87.

Examines conditions under which confidence estimation facilitates problem solving. Participants who used a confidence estimation procedure and whose teacher valued and nurtured warranted uncertainty performed better on spelling and improved more than did other participants. Sex differences are discussed.

438. Spillman, C.V., & Lutz, J.P. (1985). Criteria for successful

experiences in kindergarten. **Contemporary Education, 56**(2), 109-13.

Reports results of a study comparing performances of kindergarten tasks by early entrants to kindergarten and regular-age entrants. Sex differences are discussed.

439. Stipek, D.J. (1984). Sex differences in children's attributions for success and failure on math and spelling tests. **Sex Roles: A Research Journal, 11**(11-12), 969-81.

Reports results of a study in which students (grades five through six) were given questionnaires assessing actual performance, subjective ratings of success or failure, and performance expectations for future tests in math and spelling. Boys were more likely than girls to attribute math success to ability, but not failure to lack of ability.

440. Thomas, N.G., & Berk, L.E. (1981). Effects of school environments on the development of young children's creativity. **Child Development, 52**(4), 1153-62.

Examines effect of three types of school environment (informal, intermediate, and formal) on changes in figural creativity over a school year for first- and second-grade children. Sex differences are discussed.

441. Townley, K., & Thornburg, K.R. (1980). Maturation of the concept of death in elementary school children. **Educational Research Quarterly, 5**(2), 17-24.

Reports results of structured interviews used to ascertain level of understanding of concept of death in 52 elementary school children. Data analysis showed sex, religious affiliation, and death of a close relative had little or no relationship to level of understanding of death.

442. Vasta, R., et al. (1980). Sex differences in pattern copying: spatial cues or motor skills? **Child Development, 51**(3), 932-34.

Reports results of astudy of the accuracy of pattern copying by male and female 10-year-olds. Contrary to expectations, independent of the stimulus size, males benefited from spatial response cues whereas females did not.

443. Wapner, J.G., & Connor, K. (1986). The role of defensiveness in cognitive impulsivity. **Child Development, 57**(6), 1370-74.

Reports results of a study involving 56 boys and 64 girls ranging in age from 9 to 11 years, approximately, showing significant and positive correlation of defensiveness and impulsivity among boys, both directly and indirectly. Defensiveness does not contribute to impulsivity for girls either directly or indirectly, although test anxiety correlates with girls' impulsivity.

444. Ziviani, J., & Elkins, J. (1984). An evaluation of handwriting performance. **Educational Review, 36**(3), 249-61.

The legibility components (letter formation, spacing, alignment, and size) and speed of handwriting were assessed for children in grades three to seven. In general, interrater and test-retest reliabilities are higher for older children. Girls wrote significantly faster and smaller and made fewer errors in letter formation than boys.

Music and Art

445. Baker, D.S. (1980). The effect of appropriate and inappropriate in-class song performance models on performance preference of third- and fourth-grade students. **Journal of Research in Music Education, 28**(1), 3-17.

Reports results of a study showing performance preferences and students' ideas of "correct" performance affected by appropriate and inappropriate models. A slight difference is shown between boys and girls and an overall preference for fast/loud music over slow/soft music.

446. Brown, E.V. (1984). Developmental characteristics of clay figures made by children: 1970 to 1981. **Studies in Art Education, 26**(1), 56-60.

Replication of a 1970 investigation of the characteristics of clay figures made by children from ages 5 to 11 in order to determine whether children were more adept than 10 years before. Methods of construction and amount of detail in the second study varied from the earlier one. Sex differences are discussed.

447. Davidson, C.W., & Powell, L.A. (1986). The effects of easy-listening background music on the on-task-performance of fifth grade children. **Journal of Educational Research, 80**(1) 29-33.

Reports results of the effect of background music on-task performance. Fifth grade science students were observed for 42 class sessions over a four-month period. Time-series analyses indicate a significant increase for male subjects and for the total class.

448. Hedden, S.K. (1982). Prediction of music achievement in the elementary school. **Journal of Research in Music Education, 30**(1), 61-68.

Reports results of a study examining predictors of music achievement for general music students in upper elementary grades. Predictors examined were attitude toward music, self-concept in music, music background, academic achievement, and gender. Sex differences are discussed.

449. LeBlanc, A., & Sherrill, C. (1986). Effect of vocal vibrato and performer's sex on children's music preference. **Journal of Research in Music Education, 34**(4), 222-37.

Reports results of a study investigating effect of low and high levels of vocal vibrato, employed by male and female performers, on self-reported music listening preferences of upper elementary school children. Results show significant preference for low levels of vibrato and male singers.

450. May, W.V. (1985). Musical style preferences and aural discrimination skills of primary grade school children. **Journal of Research in Music Education, 33**(1), 7-22.

Reports results of a study in which most primary-grade children were found to prefer current popular musical styles--rock, country and western, and easy listening pop to other kinds of music. Music preferences of males and females generally are the same.

451. McCarthy, J.F. (1980). Individualized instruction, student achievement, and dropout in an urban elementary instrumental music program. **Journal of Research in Music Education, 28**(1), 59-69.

Reports results of a study demonstrating that an individualized technique was as effective as more traditional types of ensemble instruction in developing music reading skills for beginning instrumentalists. Findings show no significant effect on achievement or dropout from the program by differences between teachers or differences of sex or socioeconomic status of students.

452. Neperud, R.W., et al. (1986). Ethnic aesthetics: the meaning of ethnic art for blacks and nonblacks. **Studies in Art Education, 28**(1), 16-29.

Assesses differences in blacks' and nonblacks' rating of representational and nonrepresentational art works by black and nonblack artists. Results suggest ethnic identity in art does not ensure aesthetic valuing by ethnic groups. Sex differences are discussed.

453. Pogonowski, L.M. (1985). Attitude assessment of upper elementary students in a process-oriented music curriculum. **Journal of Research in Music Education, 33**(4), 247-57.

Reports results of a study of fourth- through sixth-grade students, assessing relationship between classroom music attitudes and grade level, gender, and socioeconomic level. Results show little relationship between classroom music attitudes and musical aptitude.

454. Ramsey, I.L. (1982). Effect of art style on children's picture preferences. **Journal of Educational Research, 75**(4), 237-40.

Reports results of a study measuring and correlating children's preferences for different art styles with text content and sex. Results indicate content influences style preference, but sex seems to make no difference.

455. Schleuter, S.L., & Schleuter, L.J. (1985). The relationship of grade level and sex differences to certain rhythmic responses of primary grade children. **Journal of Research in Music Education, 33**(1), 23-29.

Results show verbal chanting as the most accurate response for kindergarten students and, along with clapping, for first graders.

Clapping is shown as most accurate for third graders and, along with chanting, for second graders. Overall, stepping response was the least accurate. Girls consistently received higher mean scores than boys.

456. Schmidt, C.P., & Sinor, J. (1986). An investigation of the relationships among music audiation, musical creativity, and cognitive style. **Research in Music Education, 34**(3), 160-72.

Investigates achievement in convergent and divergent musical tasks as a function of the cognitive style dimension of reflection/impulsivity among second graders. Significant relationships are shown for cognitive style and gender on measures of tone, rhythm, and creative music thinking.

Peer Relations | Peer Evaluations

457. Adams, G.R. (1983). Social competence during adolescence: social sensitivity, locus of control, empathy, and peer popularity. **Journal of Youth and Adolescence, 12**(3), 203-11.

Reports results of a study of male and female adolescents concerning predictive relationship between social competency and peer relations and age differences in social competence. Based upon a social deficit hypotheses, linear age differences are reported in social knowledge, locus of control, and a trend in empathy.

458. Ahlgren, A., & Johnson, D.W. (1979). Sex differences in cooperative and competitive attitudes from the 2nd through the 12th grades. **Developmental Psychology, 15**(1), 45-49.

Reports attitudinal data from a survey of students in grades 2-12 used to depict sex differences in cooperativeness and competitiveness in a natural school setting.

459. Barclay, J.R., & Kehle, T.J. (1979). The impact of handicapped students on other students in the classroom. **Journal of Research and Development in Education, 12**(4), 80-92.

Summarizes three studies using Barclay Classroom Climate Inventory to measure psychological and social-affective impact of six classroom settings and a specific mainstreaming procedure on educable mentally retarded and learning disabled pupils. Sex differences are discussed.

460. Barnett, M.A., et al. (1979). Relationship between competitiveness and empathy in 6- and 7-year-olds. **Developmental Psychology, 15**(2), 221-22.

Reports results of administering the Feshbach and Roe test of empathy to children aged 6 and 7 years while they were preparing either to compete or to cooperate with another child on a game. Sex differences are discussed.

461. Berndt, T.J. (1981). Effects of friendship on prosocial intentions and behavior. **Child Development, 52**(20), 636-43.

Reports results of a study of kindergarten pupils, second graders, and fourth graders assessing (1) prosocial intentions toward a friend in everyday life situations, (2) prosocial behavior toward a friend in tasks where sharing leads to decreases in one's own and relative gains, and (3) sex differences in the effects of friendship on prosocial intentions and behavior.

462. Busse, T.V., & Seraydarian, L. (1979). First names and popularity in grade school children. **Psychology in the Schools, 16**(1), 149-53.

Reports results of a study of relationships between first name desirability and popularity using boys and girls from six elementary schools. Girls' popularity, as demonstrated by positive sociometric choices, was significantly related to desirability of their first names. Findings show some indication that boys' popularity with girls was influenced by boys' first names.

463. Chafel, J.A. (1988). Social comparisons by children: an analysis of research on sex differences. **Sex Roles: A Journal of Research, 18**(7-8), 461-87.

Analyzes research on social comparisons by children of elementary school age or younger with respect to sex differences. Categorizes research by investigation setting, summarizes major findings, and makes recommendations for future research.

464. Downing, L.L., & Bothwell, K.H., Jr. (1979). Open-space schools: anticipation of peer interaction and development of cooperative interdependence. **Journal of Educational Psychology, 71**(4), 478-84.

Reports results of administering the Prisoner's Dilemma Game and locus of control measures to eighth graders enrolled in an open or closed space school. Open-space students developed cooperative interdependence and made seating choices indicative of anticipated peer interaction most frequently. Interactions involving sex and race are reported for cooperation and locus of control.

465. Evans, J., & Roberts, G.C. (1987). Physical competence and the development of children's peer relations. **Quest, 39**(1), 23-35.

A review of literature on physical competence and peer relations that concludes that physically competent children acquire more status and enjoy greater social success than do physically inept children. Sex differences are discussed.

466. Friedman, P. (1980). Racial preferences and identifications of white elementary schoolchildren. **Contemporary Educational Psychology, 5**(3), 256-65.

Examines racial preferences and identifications of white children in both a white monoracial and a multiracial setting using a doll selection procedure. A majority of children preferred white over comparable black dolls. However, more black doll selections were made in multiracial than in monoracial schools. Sex differences are discussed.

467. Hazzard, A. (1983). Children's experience with, knowledge of, and attitude toward disabled persons. **Journal of Special Education, 17**(2), 131-39.

Reports children's knowledge increased with age but was unrelated to sex or previous experience with disabled persons. In contrast, children's social-distance ratings are shown as unrelated to age but vary with previous experience and sex. Children with more experience and girls expressed greater willingness to interact with disabled peers.

468. Henton, J., et al. (1983). Romance and violence in dating relationships. **Journal of Family Issues, 4**(3), 467-82.

Reports of a survey of high school students to investigate violence between dating couples. Findings show males more accepting of violence in dating and marriage than females.

469. Hughes, R., Jr., et al. (1981). Development of empathic understanding in children. **Child Development, 52**(1), 122-28.

Assesses boys' and girls' understanding of emotions of others and of their own emotional reactions to emotion in others.

470. Langlois, J.H., & Styczynski, L.E. (1979). The effects of physical attractiveness on the behavior attributions and peer preferences of acquainted children. **International Journal of Behavioral Development, 2**(4), 325-41.

Investigates age-dependent differences in relationship between physical attractiveness and social perceptions of acquainted classmates. Sex differences are discussed.

471. Luftig, R.L. (1987). Children's loneliness, perceived ease in making friends and estimated social adequacy: development and social metacognition. **Child Study Journal, 17**(1), 35-53.

Investigates the extent of children's loneliness, their perceived ease in making friends, their estimated social competence as a function of grade and sex, and their preferences concerning eight childhood activities.

472. Maccoby, E.E., & Jacklin, C.N. (1980). Sex differences in aggression: a rejoinder and reprise. **Child Development, 51**(4), 964-80.

Evidence from cross-cultural studies and observational studies support contentions that males are more aggressive than females as early as preschool.

473. Markus, E.J., & Barasch, M. (1982). Assessing ethnic integration in the classroom. **Journal of Research and Development in Education, 15**(2), 1-10.

Attempts to develop an instrument for assessing social integration of ethnic groups in the classroom. Sociometric questionnaires were used to ask second-grade students to choose classmates whose company they most preferred. Preliminary findings indicated that gender is a more divisive factor within the classroom than ethnicity.

474. Peeler, E., & Rimmer, S.M. (1981). The Assertiveness Scale for Children. **Elementary School Guidance and Counseling, 16**(1), 43-46.

Describes an assertiveness scale for children developed to assess four dimensions of assertiveness across three categories of interpersonal situations. The scale was administered to elementary and middle school children and re-administered to assess test-retest reliability. Test-retest reliability was low while internal consistency reliability was acceptable. Sex differences are discussed.

475. Plummer, D.L., & Graziano, W.G. (1987). Impact of grade retention on the social development of elementary school children. **Development Psychology, 23**(2), 267-75.

Explores impact of peers on retained students. Second- and fifth-grade retained and nonretained children provided measures of peer reward allocations, preferences for social and task partners, attitudes about school environment, report card expectancy, and self-esteem. Peer discrimination was moderated by the rater's age, gender, physical size, and retention status.

476. Richey, M.H., & Richey, H.W. (1980). The significance of

best-friend relationships in adolescence. **Psychology in the Schools, 17**(4). 536-40.

Female relationships are reported as more intense, demonstrative, exclusive, and nurturant than male relationships which are more likely to be based on enjoyable companionship and similarity in attitudes.

477. Rogosch, F.A., & Newcomb, A.F. (1989). Children's perceptions of peer reputations and their social reputations among peers. **Child Development, 60**(3), 597-610.

Reports assessment of the influence of social and cognitive developmental processes on the construction of social reputation. Subjects were first-, third-, and fifth-grade boys and girls who provided free descriptions of their classmates. Sex differences are discussed.

478. Rotenberg, K.J. (1984). Sex differences in children's trust in peers. **Sex Roles: A Journal of Research, 11**(9-10), 953-57.

Children (in Grades K, 2, and 4) were required to judge how much they trusted each of their classmates. A same sex pattern of peer trust was found in fourth and second graders, but not in kindergarten children. Contrary to expectation, girls were not significantly more trusting of peers than were boys.

479. Rotenberg, K.J. (1986). Same-sex patterns and sex differences in the trust-value basis of children's friendship. **Sex Roles: A Journal of Research, 15**(11-12), 613-26.

Reports research in which a sample of fourth grade students reported the secret-sharing and promise-making behavior of classroom peers and judged those classmates on trust and friendship. Findings suggest that same-sex friendship patterns are maintained by same-sex trust patterns through infrequent secret-sharing with opposite-sex peers and the perception that opposite-sex peers break secrets more frequently.

480. Sagar, H.A., et al. (1983). Race and gender barriers:

preadolescent peer behavior in academic classrooms. **Child Development, 54**(4), 1032-40.

Observations indicate that black and white sixth-grade students interact primarily with others of their own sex and race. The study shows boys interacting more across racial lines than girls, and blacks serving as sources of interaction almost twice as much as whites.

* Simmons, R.G., et al. (1979). Entry into early adolescence: the impact of school structure, puberty, and early dating on self-esteem. **American Sociological Review.** (Cited as entry 691.)

481. Szynal-Brown, C., & Morgan, R.R. (1983). The effects of reward on tutor's behaviors in a cross-age tutoring context. **Journal of Experimental Child Psychology, 36**(2), 196-208.

Investigates third-grade boys' and girls' tutoring of first-grade boys and girls in three reward conditions: performance contingent, noncontingent reward, and no reward. Findings indicated that neither the tutor's teaching style nor the tutee's posttest performance was adversely affected by the reward. Sex differences are discussed.

482. Tieger, T. (1980). On the biological basis of sex differences in aggression. **Child Development, 51**(4), 943-63.

A critical examination of the empirical and theoretical basis for Maccoby and Jacklin's contention that males are more biologically predisposed toward aggressive behavior than females.

483. Tyne, T.F., & Geary, W. (1980). Patterns of acceptance-rejection among male-female elementary school students. **Child Study Journal, 10**(3), 179-90.

Investigates males' and females' sociometric evaluation of same- and opposite-sex elementary school classmates. Sex differences are discussed.

* Urberg, K., & Robbins, R.L. (1981). Adolescents' perceptions

of the costs and benefits associated with cigarette smoking: sex differences and peer influence. **Journal of Youth and Adolescence.** (Cited as entry 527.)

484. Victor, J.B., & Halverson, C.F., Jr. (1980). Children's friendship choices: effects of school behavior. **Psychology in the Schools, 17**(1), 409-14.

Reports results of a study testing peer acceptance as indexed by "Like to Sit By." The dimension "Good at Games" characterizes boys' choosing peers. Girls are shown preferring not to sit next to those their teachers rate as high in behavior problems.

485. Voeltz, L.M. (1980). Children's attitudes toward handicapped peers. **American Journal of Mental Deficiency, 84**(5), 455-64.

Reports results of a study showing four factors underlying respondents' attitudes: social contact willingness, deviance consequation, and two actual contact dimensions. Upper-elementary-age children, girls, and children in schools with the most contact with severely handicapped peers, expressed the most accepting attitudes.

486. Walsh, L.M., & Kurder, L.A. (1984). Developmental trends and gender differences in the relation between understanding of friendship and asociality. **Journal of Youth and Adolescence, 13**(1), 65-71.

Examines relationship between understanding of friendship and asociality in girls and boys, ages 9 to 17 years. Understanding friendship is shown as significantly related to age and sex. Difficulty in understanding components of friendship appears to be one correlate of boys' delinquent tendencies.

487. Wisely, D.W., & Morgan, S.B. (1981). Children's ratings of peers presented as mentally retarded and physically handicapped. **American Journal of Mental Deficiency, 86**(3), 281-86.

Reports results of a study of third- and sixth-grade children shown slides and tapes presenting target children as either physically nonhandicapped and nonretarded, physically handicapped only, mentally retarded only, or physically handicapped and mentally retarded. All children were rated more favorably by third graders than sixth graders and more favorably by boys than girls.

488. Wright, P.H., & Keple, T.W. (1981). Friends and parents of a sample of high school juniors: an exploratory study of relationship intensity and interpersonal rewards. **Journal of Marriage and the Family, 43**(3), 559-70.

Reports results of a study of high school juniors indicating girls had stronger and more rewarding relationships with friends of either sex than with parents, particularly fathers. Boys did not differentiate widely among the four target persons, but saw female friends as most rewarding and male friends as least rewarding.

489. Zarbatany, L., et al. (1985). Gender differences in altruistic reputation: are they artifactual? **Developmental Psychology, 21**(1), 97-101.

Reports results of testing hypothesis that sex differences in children's altruistic reputations that favor girls are due to sex-biased items found in peer-assessment measures. Gender-fair assessment of altruistic reputation was attempted through use of empirically derived examples of masculine, feminine, and gender-neutral prosocial behaviors.

Physical Well Being | Health | Sports

490. Aho, A.C., & Erickson, M.T. (1985). Effects of grade, gender, and hospitalization on children's medical fears. **Journal of Developmental and Behavioral Pediatrics, 6**(3), 146-53.

Reports results of a study of first, fourth, and seventh graders' completion of a medical fears questionnaire. Girls expressed significantly more frequent and more intense medical fears than boys. Fourth and seventh graders reported more medical fears than first graders. No effect is shown by previous hospitalization experience on frequency or intensity of fears.

491. Andres, F.F., et al. (1981). Actual and perceived strength differences. **Journal of Physical Education and Recreation, 52**(5), 20-21, 64.

Although there in little physiological evidence to suggest strength differences between prepubescent boys and girls, it is generally assumed by physical education experts and by children that such differences exist.

492. Auchincloss, E. (1989). Sports: a field of opportunity for girls. **Melpomene, 8**(1), 8-10.

Argues that sports is a vital part of the socialization process. Level and quality of participation contributes to such diverse issues as girls' mathematical ability, sense of isolation, and self-esteem.

493. Battle, J. (1981). Test-retest reliability of developmental tests of

visual-motor association. **Perceptual and Motor Skills, 52**(3), 716-18.

Reports results of a test-retest reliability study of the Developmental Tests of Visual-Motor Association. Sex differences are discussed.

494. Brunt, D., & Broadhead, G.D. (1982). Motor proficiency traits of deaf children. **Research Quarterly for Exercise and Sport, 53**(3), 236-38.

Reports results of a study of children at the Louisiana State School for the Deaf tested for motor proficiency using the Short Form of the Bruininks-Oseretsky Test of Motor Proficiency. Subjects appear to have lacked balancing skills but scored better than hearing children in visual motor control. Sex and age differences are discussed.

495. Burdine, J.N., et al. (1984). The effects of ethnicity, sex and father's occupation on heart health knowledge and nutrition behavior of school children: the Texas Youth Health Awareness Survey. **Journal of School Health, 54**(2), 87-90.

Reports results of a study of relationships among ethnicity, sex, and father's occupation with heart health knowledge and nutrition behavior among seventh- and eighth-graders. Findings indicate a strong need for heart health education and for culturally relevant nutrition education.

496. Charlop, M., & Atwell, C.W. (1980). The Charlop-Atwell Scale of Motor Coordination: a quick and easy assessment of young children. **Perceptual and Motor Skills, 50**(3), pt2, 1291-1308.

Describes the development and validation of the Charlop-Atwell Scale of Motor Coordination, designed to measure some aspects of the gross motor coordination of children ages 4 and 6. Test itself and scoring ranges for boys and girls are appended.

497. Chelladurai, P., & Arnott, M. (1985). Decision styles in

coaching: preferences of basketball players. **Research Quarterly for Exercise and Sport, 56**(1), 15-24.

Investigates basketball players' preferences for different decision making styles in varying situations. While females are reported as more oriented toward participation than males, preferences of both groups are seen as more influenced by main effects of coach's information and the interaction of quality requirement with problem complexity.

498. Del Greco, L., et al. (1986). Four-year results of a youth smoking prevention program using assertiveness training. **Adolescence, 21**(83), 631-40.

Seventh graders participated in health education classes consisting of either an innovative smoking education program, the program plus assertiveness training, or a traditional smoking education program. Data collected four years later reveals no significant differences in smoking behavior, changes in assertion, or sex differences among groups.

499. Draper, T.W., & Munoz, M.M. (1982). Minor physical anomalies, footprints, and behavior: was the Buddha right? **Perceptual and Motor Skills, 54**(2), 455-59.

Reports results of a study of a relationship between anomaly of footprint suggested by ancient Abhidhamma meditations and Minor Physical Anomalies Scale in children. Footprint anomalies were correlated with activity levels of children in the same way as scores on the scale and consistently with prior research using the scale. Sex differences are discussed.

500. Duncan, P.D., et al. (1985). The effects of pubertal timing on body image, school behavior, and deviance. **Journal of Youth and Adolescence, 14**(3), 227-35.

Investigates data from the National Health Examination Survey, a national probability sample of children and youth aged 12-17, to assess relationships between maturational timing and body image, school behavior, and deviance. Sex differences are discussed.

501. Engs, R.C. (1985). Health concerns over time: the apparent stability. **Health Education, 16**(3), 3-6.

Reports results of a study to determine the health concerns of students enrolled in personal health classes, to compare the results with earlier studies that used the same instrument, and to investigate the effect of gender on health concerns. Sex differences are discussed.

502. Gallagher, S.S., et al. (1984). The incidence of injuries among 87,000 Massachusetts children and adolescents: results of the 1980-81 Statewide Childhood Injury Prevention Program Surveillance System. **American Journal of Public Health, 74**(12), 1340-47.

Analysis of data on injuries among 0-19 year-olds shows that injury rates varied considerably by age, sex, and level of severity. Overall, results show that both morbidity and mortality must be considered when determining prevention priorities and that prevention efforts must be expanded to target injuries of higher incidence among adolescents. Sex differences are discussed.

503. Greendorfer, S.L., & Ewing, M.E. (1981). Race and gender differences in children's socialization into sport. **Research Quarterly for Exercise and Sport, 52**(3), 301-10.

Reports results of a study of sport socialization of children between ages of nine and 12 indicating white children are influenced by specific agents of socialization such as fathers and teachers, while black children are influenced by situational and contextual variables. Noteworthy is predominantly same-sex influence on children regardless of race.

504. Griffin, P.S. (1985). Girls' and boys' participation styles in middle school physical education team sport classes: a description and practical applications. **Physical Educator, 42**(1), 3-8.

Describes boys' and girls' participation patterns in physical education classes and discusses the practical application of this information to teaching coed physical education team sport classes.

505. Hall, E.G., & Lee, A.M. (1984). Sex differences in motor performance of young children: fact or fiction? **Sex Roles: A Journal of Research, 10**(3-4), 217-30.

Reports results of AAHPER Youth Fitness Test (1977,1978,1979) administered to third-, fourth-, and fifth-grade children who had participated for one or more years in a coeducational physical fitness program. Females consistently performed as well or better than males at the same grade level.

506. Hall, E.G., & Lee, A.M. (1981). Sex and birth order in children's goal setting and actual performance of a gross motor task. **Perceptual and Motor Skills, 53**(2), 663-66.

Investigates the effect of birth order and sex on goal setting and actual performance by elementary school boys and girls on a ring-toss task. Results indicate that firstborn boys set higher goals and perform significantly better than later-born boys, firstborn girls, or later-born girls.

507. Halverson, L.E., et al. (1982). Development of the overarm throw: movement and ball velocity changes by seventh grade. **Research Quarterly for Exercise and Sport, 53**(3), 198-205.

Reports results of a study to clarify patterns in the rate of motor development. Children observed between kindergarten and second grade were refilmed, performing an overarm throw, when they became seventh-graders. Results were compared with predictions made earlier. Differences in the skill levels of boys and girls and differences in their throwing experience are reported.

508. Halverson, L.E., & Williams, K. (1985). Developmental sequences for hopping over distance: a prelongitudinal screening. **Research Quarterly for Exercise and Sport, 56**(1), 37-44.

Reports results of tests of proposed developmental steps for hopping over distance to determine their comprehensiveness and accuracy. The pattern of sex differences is consistent with earlier research.

509. Hart, E.J., & Behr, M.T. (1980). The effects of educational intervention & parental support on dental health. **Journal of School Health, 50**(10), 572-76.

Reports results of a study to determine effectiveness of a school-based dental health education program which included a parental support component. Sex differences are discussed.

510. Hastad, D.N., & Pangrazi, R.P. (1983). Summer alterations in youth fitness. **Physical Educator, 40**(2), 81-87.

Investigates changes in children's physical fitness during summer vacation. Findings show children's cardiorespiratory fitness decreased, as did body weight, especially for boys.

511. Hensley, L.D., et al. (1982). Body fatness and motor performance during preadolescence. **Research Quarterly for Exercise and Sport, 53**(2), 133-40.

Investigates relationship between selected physical performance tests and body fatness in 563 boys and girls in grades one through four. Findings indicate that, although inversely related to the ability to move total body weight, body fatness was of minimal importance in explaining sex-based performance differences.

* Heston, M., et al. (1986). Reliability of selected measures of movement control and force production on children four through ten years of age. **Physical Educator.** (Cited as entry 159.)

512. Hoferek, M.J. (1982). Sex role prescriptions and attitudes of physical educators. **Sex Roles: A Journal of Research, 8**(1), 83-98.

Reports results of a study to explore the relationship between sex role perceptions of physical educators and their attitudes/expectations regarding female participation and performance in various physical activities. Also examines sex of teachers versus teachers' self-definition of their sex role as a determinant of curriculum objectives valued.

* Holcomb, C.A. (1981). My daughter wants to be a nurse: occupational stereotyping in health textbooks. **Journal of School Health.** (Cited as entry 54.)

513. Isaacs, L.D. (1980). Effects of ball size, ball color, and preferred color on catching by young children. **Perceptual and Motor Skills, 51**(2), 583-86.

Reports results of a study in which 45 children, ages seven to eight, were required to catch playground balls of various sizes and colors. Although the main effect for color was nonsignificant, children caught preferred-color balls significantly better than others. Males caught better than females.

514. Kisabeth, K.L. (1986). Basic instruction programs: a search for personal meaning. **Physical Educator, 43**(3), 150-54.

Examines patterns of participants' movement, purpose, and values to text differences in value due to gender, type of activity, and skill level. Sex differences are discussed.

* Langlois, J.H., & Styczinski, L.E. (1979). The effects of physical attractiveness on the behavior attributions and peer preferences of acquainted children. **International Journal of Behavioral Development.** (Cited as entry 470.)

515. Martens, F.L. (1979). A scale for measuring attitude toward physical education in the elementary school. **Journal of Experimental Education, 47**(3), 239-47.

Reports development of a scale measuring attitude toward physical education for elementary school children in grades 4 to 7. No significant difference was found between sexes.

* Mercier, J.M., & Hughes, R.P. (1981). Attitudes of selected secondary students toward family planning education. **Home Economics Research Journal.** (Cited as entry 238.)

516. Morris, A.M., et al. (1982). Age and sex differences in motor performance of 3 through 6 year old children. **Research Quarterly for Exercise and Sport, 53**(3), 214-21.

Reports results of a study of children three to six years of age tested to determine relationship of age and sex to motor performance. Tests involved balancing, scrambling, catching, speed running, long jumping, and ball throwing. Although significant age and sex differences are reported, conclusion is drawn that age generally was more closely related to performance than was gender.

517. Newell-Withrow, C. (1986). Identifying health-seeking behaviors: a study of adolescents. **Adolescence, 21**(83), 641-58.

Reports findings of a study to determine how adolescents' health-seeking behaviors, which include self-management and information-seeking behaviors, differ according to age, race, socioeconomic status, gender, and religion. Findings confirm gender as a differentiating variable for performance of information-seeking behavior.

518. Petersen, A.C., & Crockett, L. (1985). Pubertal timing and grade effects on adjustment. **Journal of Youth and Adolescence, 14**(3), 191-206.

Reports effects on adjustment of biological maturation and social timing when compared using data from a longitudinal sample of young adolescents, who were followed from the sixth through eighth grades. Sex differences are discussed.

519. Peterson, F.L., Jr., & Rubinson, L. (1982). An evaluation of the effects of the American Dental Associations's Dental Health Education Program on the knowledge, attitudes and health

locus of control of high school students. **Journal of School Health, 52**(1), 63-69.

Evaluates the effectiveness of secondary dental health education and examines the correlations among students' dental knowledge, attitudes, and health locus of control. Sex differences are discussed.

520. Placek, J., et al. (1982). Academic learning time (ALT-PE) in a traditional elementary physical education setting: a descriptive analysis. **Journal of Classroom Interaction, 17**(2), 41-47.

Reports results of a study analyzing an elementary school physical educator's interactions with students, using the Academic Learning Time-Physical Education instrument. Data were collected to show differences in learning opportunities: (1) for girls and boys; (2) for high, medium, and low ability students; and (3) in different instructional units.

521. Riggs, R.S., & Noland, M.P. (1984). Factors relation to the health knowledge and health behavior of disadvantaged black youth. **Journal of School Health, 54**(11), 431-34.

Disadvantaged black adolescents were surveyed regarding health knowledge, health locus of control, and health practices. Significant differences are shown for scores on the health knowledge test by sex, age, and health locus of control.

522. Rogers, M., et al. (1981). Cooperative games as an intervention to promote cross-racial acceptance. **American Educational Research Journal, 18**(4), 513-16.

Reports results of a study showing more cross-racial interaction among boys because they participate in more team sports. Findings indicate that cooperative games have a strong potential for facilitating social acceptance among desegregated elementary school girls. Observations of cross-racial prosocial and antagonistic interactions reveal practical value of games for increasing intergroup attraction.

523. Sexton, L.C., & Treloar, J.H. (1979). Auditory and visual perception, sex, and academic aptitude as predictors of achievement for first-grade children. **Measurement and Evaluation in Guidance, 12**(3), 140-45.

Explores relationships among visual and auditory perception, academic aptitude, sex, and school achievement. Results indicate visual perception added significantly to prediction of achievement beyond that available through knowledge of a participant's sex and academic aptitude.

524. Snow, C.E., et al. (1986). Learning to play doctor: effects of sex, age, and experience in hospital. **Discourse Processes, 9**(4), 461-73.

Indicates a greater effect of hospitalization experience on children's general conception of hospital roles and plots than on specific linguistic markers of the sick-room register. Girls performed better in the role of nurse and mother whereas boys performed relatively better in the role of doctor and father.

525. Stephenson, C. (1983). Visits by elementary school children to the school nurse. **Journal of School Health, 53**(10), 594-99.

A school nurse recorded the characteristics of elementary school children who visited her office over a six-month period. Observations show that: (1) health-seeking behavior is a learned process; (2) no differences were apparent in how often boys or girls visited the office; and (3) recurrent health problems contributed to visit frequency.

526. Umansky, W., & Cohen, L.R. (1980). Race and sex differences on the McCarthy Screening Test. **Psychology in the Schools, 17**(1), 400-04.

Reports strong trends in a study showing that with the exception of leg coordination, white subjects scored better than non-white subjects on all subtests. White females and non-white females were superior to male counterparts.

527. Urberg, K., & Robbins, R.L. (1981). Adolescents' perceptions of the costs and benefits associated with cigarette smoking: sex differences and peer influence. **Journal of Youth and Adolescence, 10**(5), 353-61.

Reports results of cigarette smoking habits among adolescents. Data shows girls view smoking as a sign of rebellion or autonomy, while boys view smoking as a social coping mechanism. Boys were more influenced than girls by their friends who smoke.

528. Villimez, C., et al. (1986). Sex differences in the relation of children's height and weight to academic performance and others' attributions of competence. **Sex Roles, 15**(11-12), 667-81.

Examines the relation of elementary school girls' and boys' height and weight to: (1) teachers and peers' perceptions of the children's independence and academic, athletic, and social competence and (2) children's achievement test scores and grades. Discusses results in relation to cultural stereotypes and their implications for child development.

529. Waber, D.P., et al. (1985). Physical maturation rate and cognitive performance in early adolescence: a longitudinal examination. **Developmental Psychology, 21**(4), 666-81.

Reports results of a longitudinal study examining (1) development of relationship between physical maturation rate and cognitive performance as children become adolescent, and (2) specific components of cognitive processing linked to physical maturation-related differences in performance on cognitive ability tasks. Differences are shown on cognitive process tasks. Sex differences are discussed.

School Attendance | Dropouts

530. Bennett, C., & Harris, J.J. III. (1982). Suspensions and expulsions of male and black students: a case study of the causes of disproportionality. **Urban Education, 16**(4), 399-423.

Reports results of a study of student, school, and staff characteristics in order to determine factors related to the disproportionate numbers of male and black students suspended or expelled from school. School practices and conditions said to mediate the problem are identified. Sex differences are discussed.

531. Bickel, F., & Qualls, R. (1980). The impact of school climate on suspension rates in the Jefferson County Public Schools. **Urban Review, 12**(2), 79-86.

Reports use of observations and questionnaires used to explore attitudes and behaviors of school staff that might influence student behavior differentially in secondary schools with high and low suspension rates. Students, teachers, and administrators in low suspension schools all judged school climate more positively than did their counterparts in high suspension schools. Sex differences are discussed.

532. Easton, J.Q., & Engelhard, G., Jr. (1982). A longitudinal record of elementary school absence and its relationship to reading achievement. **Journal of Educational Research, 75**(5), 269-74.

Reports analysis of longitudinal data on student absence rates from kindergarten through eighth grade. Findings show absence correlated significantly with teacher-assigned reading grades and standardized test scores. Sex differences are discussed.

533. Farnworth, M., et al. (1985). Preschool intervention, school success and delinquency in a high-risk sample of youth. **American Educational Research Journal, 22**(3), 445-64.

Using multiple regression analysis, the associations of delinquency with IQ and achievement scores, general school success, school attachment, preschool intervention and gender are explored for a group of high-risk black students. Sex differences are discussed.

534. Fuller, B. (1983). Youth job structure and school enrollment, 1890-1920. **Sociology of Education, 56**(3), 145-56.

Explanations of growth in American school enrollment point to rural-cultural beliefs or urban-economic antecedents. The influence of job opportunity structure on school enrollment is discussed separately for states and cities and between males and females. Both explanations are found to have validity, but more research on regional variation is needed.

535. Hewitt, J.D., & Johnson, W.S. (1979). Dropping out in "Middletown." **High School Journal, 62**(6), 252-56.

Explores reasons for the high school dropout rate at four different times (1924, 1937, 1952, 1977) in Muncie, Indiana. Sex differences are discussed.

536. Parcel, G.S., et al. (1979). A comparison of absentee rates of elementary schoolchildren with asthma and nonasthmatic schoolmates. **Pediatrics, 64**(6), 878-81.

Compares school absence in children known to have asthma with a random sample of nonasthmatic elementary school children. Findings show children with asthma have significantly higher absentee rate than do nonasthmatic children. Sex differences are discussed.

537. Tidwell, R. (1988). Dropouts speak out: qualitative data on early school departures. **Adolescence, 23**(92), 939-954.

Reports results of home interviews with urban high school dropouts concerning their primary reason for leaving school early. Female and male respondents of 5 ethnic groups (Native Americans, Asians, blacks, Hispanics, and whites) answered questions concerning their dropout history. Reasons given for leaving school before graduating include boredom, poor grades, and home/family responsibilities. In general, ethnic and sex group differences in the dropout experience are noted.

School Settings

* Atkinson, D.R., & Dorsey, M.F. (1979). The effects of counseling for conformity or social change on perceived counselor credibility. **Journal of Counseling Services.** (Cited as entry 172.)

538. Brophy, J.E., et al. Grade level and sex of student as context variables in elementary school. **Journal of Classroom Interaction, 14**(2), 11-17.

Reports results of a study showing that grade level and sex of student are important variables determining teacher attitudes and responses.

539. Bryant, J., et al. (1981). Ridicule as an educational corrective. **Journal of Educational Psychology, 73**(5), 722-27.

One of the three motivators (ridicule, insult, gentle reminder) was included in a handout of course reading assignments. Although the gentle reminder and insult increased test scores somewhat, only ridicule produced a significant increase in information acquisition. Sex differences were found for the insult versus ridicule conditions.

540. Buffington, P.W., & Stilwell, W.E. (1981). Teachers' attitudes and affective education: an unexpected finding. **Education, 102**(2), 176-82.

In a self-control and competency study of subjects using different treatments compared across gender, grade, and teachers, data suggests teacher attitudes toward male students changed as a result of affective modules. Results also replicate findings that, overall, teachers rate females higher than males.

541. Center, D.B., & Wascom, A.L. (1987). Teacher perceptions of social behavior in behaviorally disordered and socially normal children and youth. **Behavioral Disorders, 12**(3), 200-06.

Compares teacher perceptions of either behaviorally disordered or socially normal students and reports that teachers perceive more prosocial behavior by normal, female, and older subjects. Data also show teachers perceived an increase in negative social behavior for normal secondary-age students but not for behaviorally disordered students.

542. Christie, D.J., & Glickman, C.D. (1980). The effects of classroom noise on children: evidence for sex differences. **Psychology in the Schools, 17**(1), 405-08.

Reports results of a study in which children worked on a matrix task in either a noisy or quiet environment. Performance on the intellectual task increased with age. In environment with classroom noise, boys consistently solved more complex matrix problems than girls.

543. Clarricoates, K. (1981). The experience of patriarchal schooling. **Interchange on Educational Policy, 12**(2-3), 185-205.

Reports methods whereby female students are socialized into more typical roles by patriarchal schooling: (1) the organization and structure of the school; (2) biased curriculum materials; and (3) distinctions based on gender in the classroom.

544. Colton, J.A., & White, M.A. (1985). High school student satisfaction and perceptions of the school environment. **Contemporary Educational Psychology, 10**(3), 235-48.

Reports use of the instrument "Students and Their Schools" to assess perceived availability and value of different academic and interpersonal dimensions of the high school environment and student satisfaction with them. Sex differences are discussed.

545. Cornbleth, C., & Korth, W. (1980). Teacher perceptions and teacher-student interaction in integrated classrooms. **Journal of Experimental Education, 48**(4), 259-63.

Reports results of a study of teacher ratings of students' potential achievement, classroom behavior, personal characteristics, and teacher-student dyadic interaction measures. Examines nature of teacher perceptions and interaction with black and white, male and female students in integrated classrooms. Sex differences are discussed.

546. Crockenberg, S.B., & Bryant, B.K. (1979). Individualized learning environments: intra- and interpersonal consequences. **Journal of School Psychology, 17**(1), 17-26.

Examines the effects of individual goal structures on the intra- and interpersonal behavior of 120 fourth-grade children. Findings show both boys and girls appeared to adopt the evaluations of their work given by the experimenter and appeared to be influenced thereby in later prize-giving to themselves and to others.

547. Croll, P. (1985). Teacher interaction with individual male and female pupils in junior-age classrooms. **Educational Research, 27**(3), 220-23.

Reports results of a study showing that boys receive a higher average level of individual attention from their teachers but that the difference between boys and girls is much less dramatic than is sometimes claimed. The researcher suggests the imbalance may be a problem of classroom management rather than of sexist bias.

548. Daly, J.A., & Suite, A. (1981). Classroom seating choice and teacher perceptions of students. **Journal of Experimental Education, 50**(2), 64-69.

Investigates impact of seat position on teachers' initial judgments of students. Students sitting forward in the classroom were regarded more favorably than those at the rear. Results indicate a significant effect for seating and a three-way interaction between chosen seat, sex, and grade.

549. Driscoll, A., et al. (1985). Student reports for primary teacher evaluation. **Educational Research Quarterly**, **9**(3), 43-50.

Reports the results of administering the Primary Grade Pupil Report to kindergarten through second-grade students, who rated their teachers according to whether their teachers were like the statement. Sex differences are discussed.

550. Dusek, J.B., & Joseph, G. (1983). The bases of teacher expectancies: a meta-analysis. **Journal of Educational Psychology**, **75**(3), 327-46.

Reports results of a meta-analysis of 77 studies on teacher expectancies. Included are student attractiveness, conduct, cumulative folder information, race, and social class. Student gender and the number of parents at home are not shown as related to teacher expectancies.

551. Epstein, M.H., et al. (1986). Teacher ratings of hyperactivity in learning-disabled, emotionally disturbed, and mentally retarded children. **Journal of Special Education**, **20**(2), 219-29.

Teachers of learning disabled, behavior disordered, educational mentally retarded, and non-handicapped students ages 6-18 rated their students on the Abbreviated Teacher Rating Scale, a measure used to assess hyperactivity. Prevalence, distribution, and patterns of hyperactivity are analyzed, as well as age and sex differences. Cross-cultural comparisons are noted.

552. Fagot, B.I. (1981). Male and female teachers: do they treat boys and girls differently? **Sex Roles: A Journal of Research**, **7**(3), 263-71.

Reports results of a study of experienced and inexperienced teachers, male and female, observed in preschool classes to determine (1) what determines differential responses to boys and girls with regard to sex-preferred behaviors, and (2) whether male and female teachers differ in their teaching styles.

553. French, J. (1984). Gender imbalances in the primary classroom: an interactional account. **Educational Research, 26**(2), 127-36.

A verbatim transcription of a lesson in a class of 10- to 11-year-olds is analyzed to support the observation that, in mixed-sex classrooms, male pupils receive more teacher attention than females. Among the reasons found for this imbalance is the tendency of boys to engage in attention getting strategies.

554. Good, T.L., et al. (1980). Classroom interaction as a function of teacher expectations, student sex, and time of year. **Journal of Educational Psychology, 72**(3), 378-85.

Reports results of a study of classroom interaction patterns between male and female students perceived as either high or low achievers. Expectation and sex results were consistent with previous findings.

555. Guskey, T.R. (1981). Measurement of the responsibility teachers assume for academic successes and failures in the classroom. **Journal of Teacher Education, 32**(3), 44-51.

Reports development and validation of a scale assessing teacher beliefs concerning responsibility for student academic success. Results show striking difference in male/female teacher responses: female teachers consistently assumed greater responsibility for the learning outcomes of their students.

556. Guskey, T.R. (1982). Differences in teachers' perceptions of personal control of positive versus negative student learning outcomes. **Contemporary Educational Psychology, 7**(1), 70-80.

Reports that the causal attributions of 184 teachers from metropolitan school districts varied with positive versus negative learning outcomes both for internality/externality and stability of cause. Relations to overall efficacy, teaching experience, grade level taught, and teacher gender are examined. Sex differences are discussed.

557. Gustafson, G.E. (1987). The effects of socioeconomic and demographic characteristics on the public's assessment of the schools. **Spectrum, 5**(4), 3-6.

Examines relationship of certain socioeconomic and demographic characteristics (parent/nonparent, education level, age, gender, city size, religious preference, and geographic region) to a community's assessment of public school education.

558. Haladyna, T., & Thomas, G. (1979). The attitudes of elementary school children toward school and subject matters. **Journal of Experimental Education, 48**(1), 18-23.

Investigates attitudes of elementary and junior high school students toward school and toward seven subjects as a function of grade level and sex. Findings show attitudes decline in higher grades, sex differences are reflected in attitudes, and negative attitudes exist toward social studies.

559. Harris, M.J., et al. (1986). The effects of teacher expectations, gender, and behavior on pupil academic performance and self-concept. **Journal of Educational Research, 79**(3), 173-79.

Ten professional and ten peer teachers were videotaped while teaching a short lesson. Detailed codings and ratings of videotapes allow an examination of interrelationships among teacher expectations, gender, teaching behaviors, and student outcome measures of cognitive performance and academic self-concept.

560. Hoge, R.D., & Butcher, R. (1984). Analysis of teacher judgments of pupil achievement levels. **Journal of Educational Psychology, 76**(5), 777-81.

Reports results of a study of twelve teachers who estimated achievement test performance, basic intellectual ability, and academic motivation of each of their pupils. Standardized reading achievement and intelligence tests were administered to the pupils. Analysis reveals a high level of accuracy for achievement judgments when assessed against test scores. Pupil gender is not shown to bias teacher judgments.

561. Horne, M.D., & Larrivee, B. (1979). Behavior rating scales: need for refining normative data. **Perceptual and Motor Skills, 49**(2), 383-88.

Reports results of a study to generate normative data by grade and sex to accompany behavior rating scales. Findings include data showing females with more positive ratings.

562. Irvine, J.J. (1985). Teacher communication patterns as related to the race and sex of the student. **Journal of Educational Research, 78**(6), 338-45.

Reports results of a study of the interactive effects of sex and race on teacher communications patterns in 67 classrooms. ANOVAs reveal two significant main effects for race, five for sex, and three significant race/sex interactions. Previous research literature is summarized.

563. Jeter, J.T., & Davis, O.L., Jr. (1982). Differential classroom interaction in social studies as a function of differential expectations of pupil achievements. **Journal of Social Studies Research, 6**(1), 1-7.

Reports results of a study investigating whether differences in teacher verbal interactions with students are a function of achievement expectations and sex differences. Ten fourth grade social studies teachers and 120 students were observed using the Brophy-Good dyadic observation system. Findings indicate that achievement expectations, but not sex, influenced teacher interactions.

564. Karper, W.B., & Martinek, T.J. (1983). The differential

influence of instructional factors on motor performance among handicapped and non-handicapped children in mainstreamed physical education classes. **Educational Research Quarterly, 8**(3), 40-46.

Reports results of a study to determine differential relationships among teacher perceptions of (1) student expression of effort; (2) teacher expectation; (3) grade; (4) school; (5) teacher; (6) sex; and (7) being handicapped/nonhandicapped on gross motor performance. Subjects were handicapped and nonhandicapped children integrated together in physical education classes.

565. Khan, N.A., & Hoge, R.D. (1983). A teacher-judgment measure of social competence: validity data. **Journal of Consulting and Clinical Psychology, 51**(6), 809-14.

Assesses the behavioral meaning of scores from a teacher-judgment measure of classroom behavior of kindergarten children. Results support the validity of teachers' judgments of interest and participation displayed by boys and cooperation and compliance displayed by girls.

566. Leinhardt, G., et al. (1979). Learning what's taught: sex differences in instruction. **Journal of Educational Psychology, 71**(4), 432-39.

Teacher interactions with second-grade students were coded to investigate sex differences in children's reading and mathematics performance. Results reveal teachers made more academic contacts with girls in reading and with boys in math and spent relatively more cognitive time with girls in reading and boys in math.

567. Lockheed, M.E. (1986). Reshaping the social order: the case of gender segregation. **Sex Roles: A Journal for Research, 14**(11-12), 617-28.

Reports results of a study of gender segregation in fourth and fifth grade classrooms. Students working in small, experimental, mixed-sex, instructional groups engaged in more cross-sex interactions than students in control groups. Boys in experimental classrooms showed greater preference for working in cross-sex groups.

568. London, C.B.G., & Griffith, A.R. (1981). Inner-city teachers and school-community relations. **Urban Education, 15**(4), 435-49.

Examines differences between black and white teachers concerning home visits, out of class contacts with students, and participation in problem situations. Also investigates whether male or female black teachers give more time to school-community organizations and who most frequently asks black teachers for advice in inner-city schools.

* Martin, S., & Cowles, M. (1983). Locus of control among children in various educational environments. **Perceptual and Motor Skills.** (Cited as entry 671.)

569. McIntyre, L.L. (1988). Teacher gender: a predictor of special education referral? **Journal of Learning Disabilities, 21**(6), 382-83.

Reports results of a crossbreak analysis showing that, when teachers consider students with high levels of problem behavior for special education referral, male teachers are less likely than female teachers to refer.

570. McTeer, J.H. (1979). Sex differences in students' interest in certain discipline areas of the social studies. **Journal of Social Studies Research, 3**(2), 58-64.

Describes a survey measuring sex differences in students' interest in five social studies discipline areas given to high school seniors in Georgia. More boys selected history as most liked and psychology/sociology as least liked, while more girls selected psychology/sociology as most liked.

571. Medway, F.J., & Egelson, R. (1980). Teacher ratings of internal and external students in open and traditional class

environments. **Psychology in the Schools, 17**(1), 390-95.

Reports results showing girls rated higher than boys and internals higher than externals on achievement and behavior. Also shows sex interacted with school environment, such that girls' achievement ratings exceeded those of boys only in open classes.

572. Osterlind, S.J. (1980). Preschool impact on children: its sustaining effects into kindergarten. **Educational Research Quarterly, 5**(4), 21-30.

Reports results of a study of children in kindergarten, comparing pupils who had previously attended preschool with those who had not. Reading (or reading readiness) and mathematics achievement, academic potential, social and emotional maturity, conformity to successful pupil behaviors, and adjustment to academic and social setting in the classroom are examined. Sex differences are discussed.

573. Pittman, R.B. (1979). Situational referents of an academic setting and locus of control. **Journal of Experimental Education, 47**(4), 290-96.

Reports results of a study of two issues: (1) students' perceptions of various situational influences of the school environment with regard to locus of control, (2) the relationship of situational influences to academic achievement. Situational influences involving parents, parental interaction, and home environment are shown related to achievement. Sex differences are discussed.

574. Pratt, D.L. (1985). Responsibility for student success/failure and observed verbal behavior among secondary science and mathematics teachers. **Journal of Research in Science Teaching, 22**(9), 807-16.

Compares selected teacher beliefs and verbal behaviors among secondary science and mathematics teachers. Teacher beliefs include teacher responsibility for student success and failure. Comparisons are made for (1) science/mathematics; (2) junior/senior high; (3) teachers of advanced/basic courses; and (4) male/female teachers.

575. Prawat, R.S., & Jarvis, R. (1980). Gender difference as a factor in teachers' perceptions of students. **Journal of Educational Psychology, 72**(6), 743-49.

Examines teacher perceptions of students as influenced by differences in student gender. Elementary school teachers' perceptions of students are assessed by their rating children in their classes on various dimensions. Results show student ability/achievement are more potent in teacher perceptions than gender.

576. Prawat, R.S., & Nickerson, J.R. (1985). The relationship between teacher thought and action and student affective outcomes. **Elementary School Journal, 85**(4), 529-40.

Results of this study do not support the hypothesis that elementary school teachers who place high priority on affective outcomes are most effective in promoting positive affect in their classrooms. Gender and race bias are discussed.

577. Sampson, J.P., Jr., & Loesch, L.C. (1980). Relationships among counselor trainees' values and counseling orientations. **Humanist Educator, 19**(1), 17-25.

Reports results of a study showing that neither personal nor interpersonal values systematically related to counseling orientation preferences of counselor trainees. No significant differences between female and male counselor trainees relative to value pattern or counseling orientation preference are reported.

578. Schlosser, L., & Algozzine, B. (1980). Sex, behavior, and teacher expectancies. **Journal of Experimental Education, 48**(3), 231-36.

Reports results of a study asking elementary school teachers to describe a third-grade child and their attitudes about working with the child, based on case reports describing either sex-consistent or inconsistent behaviors. Sex-inappropriate behavior was viewed less favorably than sex-appropriate behavior.

579. Seidman, E., et al. (1979). Assessment of classroom behavior: a multiattribute, multisource approach to instrument development and validation. **Journal of Educational Psychology, 71**(4), 451-64.

Reports development and validation of three instruments for the multidimensional assessment of a child's classroom behavior. The multidimensional nature, internal consistency, and test-retest properties of scales depicting teacher-, peer-, and self-rated behavior are explicated. Sex differences are discussed.

* Shapiro, J.E. (1980). Primary children's attitudes toward reading in male and female teachers' classrooms: an exploratory study. **Journal of Reading Behavior.** (Cited as entry 308.)

580. Simpson, A.W., & Erickson, M.T. (1983). Teachers' verbal and nonverbal communication patterns as a function of teacher race, student gender, and student race. **American Educational Research Journal, 20**(2), 183-98.

Examines the verbal and nonverbal behaviors of first-grade teachers in order to assess differences based on sex and race of child and race of teacher. Results indicate that white teachers directed more verbal praise and criticism toward black males.

581. Smith, D.K. (1981). Classroom management and consultation: implications for school psychology. **Psychology in the Schools, 18**(4), 475-81.

Analyzes approaches to classroom misbehavior by classroom teachers and graduate students completing their training in school psychology, using the induction-sensitization model of socialization. Significant differences are reported, with teachers displaying a more sensitizing (punitive) approach to classroom management. A significant gender-profession interaction was found.

* Swager, R.G. (1981). Self-disclosure and the school guidance counselor. **School Counselor.** (Cited as entry 696.)

* Thomas, N.G., & Berk, L.E. (1981). Effects of school environments on the development of young children's creativity. **Child Development.** (Cited as entry 440.)

582. Tobias, S., et al. (1983). Special education referrals: failure to replicate student-teacher ethnicity interaction. **Journal of Educational Psychology, 75**(5), 705-07.

Reports results of a study investigating influence of student sex and ethnicity, and teacher sex, ethnicity, and teaching level on referrals to special education. Responses of teachers to a systematically varied protocol show recommendations influenced by teacher ethnicity and teaching level but not by student sex or race.

* Wagenaar, T.C. (1981). High school seniors' views of themselves and their schools: a trend analysis. **Phi Delta Kappan.** (Cited as entry 698.)

583. Weis, S.F. (1979). Examinations of home economics textbooks for sex bias. **Home Economics Research Journal, 7**(3), 147-62.

Reports four analyses conducted on a sample of 100 randomly selected, secondary home economics textbooks published between 1964 and 1974. Findings indicate contents show sex bias in language usage, in pictures portraying male and female role environments, and in role behaviors and expectations emphasized.

Science

584. Anderson, C., & Butts, D. (1980). A comparison of individualized and group instruction in a sixth-grade electricity unit. **Journal of Research in Science Teaching, 17**(2), 139-45.

Reports results of a study in which worksheets were adapted from an Elementary Science Study unit, to develop an individualized set of instructional materials on electricity. Research questions were asked regarding relationships of teaching technique to achievement and attitudes, gender, and interactions of treatment and gender.

585. Baker, D.R. (1985). Predictive value of attitude, cognitive ability, and personality to science achievement in the middle school. **Journal of Research in Science Teaching, 22**(2), 103-113.

Examines relationship of attitude toward science, spatial ability, mathematical ability, and scientific personality (measured by the Myers-Briggs Type Indicator) on the achievement of eighth-grade students. Males and females with science grades of C or D had the most characteristics not associated with science.

586. Cannon, R.K., Jr., & Simpson, R.D. (1985). Relationships among attitude, motivation, and achievement of ability grouped, seventh-grade, life science students. **Science Education, 69**(2), 121-38.

Reports results of a comprehensive, longitudinal investigation examining influences on commitment to science and achievement in science among adolescent students. Findings show science attitude and achievement motivation declined throughout the year, life science achievement increased, and differences in achievement motivation occurred between female and male students.

587. Chiarelott, L., & Czerniak, C. (1987). Science anxiety: implications for science curriculum and teaching. **Clearing House, 60**(5), 202-05.

Reports results of a study of elementary and secondary school students testing science anxiety. Data shows females more anxious about studying science than males at every grade level. Links among achievement, attitudes, and science anxiety appear to be strong.

588. Craig, J., & Ayres, D. (1988). Does primary science affect girls' and boys' interest in secondary science? **School Science Review, 69**(248), 417-26.

Investigates the influence of differing elementary science experiences on the interests of girls and boys in secondary school science. Attempts to link these experiences with science performance. Focuses on the elementary experience of girls and compares the sexes.

* Donovan, E.P., et al. (1985). A new science and engineering career interest survey for middle school students. **Journal of Research in Science Teaching.** (Cited as entry 45.)

589. Doran, R.L., & Jacobson, W.J. (1984). What research says: how are our fifth graders doing? **Science and Children, 22**(1), 41-42.

Examines science achievement and attitude scores of fifth-grade students obtained from the Second International Science Study. Compares these results to those obtained from students in 1970. Data related to biology, space sciences, sex differences, and other areas are highlighted.

* Finn, J.D. (1980). Sex differences in educational outcomes: a

cross-national study. **Sex Roles: A Journal of Research.** (Cited as entry 9.)

590. Fuller, E.W., et al. (1979). The science achievement of third graders using visual, symbolic, and manipulative instructional treatments. **Journal of Research in Science Teaching, 16**(2), 129-36.

Examines the influence of gender, reading level of student, and source of data on science concept formation and retention. Results indicate reading level of students influences science concept formation and retention, but gender and source of data (method of instruction) do not.

591. Haertel, G.D., et al. (1981). Early adolescent sex differences in science learning: evidence from the National Assessment of Educational Progress. **American Educational Research Journal, 18**(3), 329-41.

Data from the 1976 NAEP Science Assessment were used to explore sex differences in science learning and its determinants with controls for ethnicity and parental socioeconomic status. No sex difference in science learning was found, but a sex-specific trend in science motivation was detected.

592. Hall, V.C., et al. (1986). Behavior, motivation, and achievement in desegregated junior high school science classes. **Journal of Educational Psychology, 78**(2), 108-115.

In an attempt to locate possible antecedents for racial differences in science achievement, measures of math and reading achievement, causal attribution, attitude toward school success, and in-class behavior were acquired from students in desegregated science classrooms. Sex differences are reported.

593. Handley, H.M., & Morse, L.W. (1984). Two-year study relating adolescents' self-concept and gender role perceptions to achievement and attitudes toward science. **Journal of Research in Science Teaching, 21**(6), 599-607.

Reports results of a study indicating that students' self-concepts and gender role perceptions were related to achievement and attitudes toward science, but more related to attitudes than achievement. In addition, relationships became more pronounced for students as they matured from seventh to eighth graders.

594. Harty, H., et al. (1987). Gender influences on concept structure interrelatedness competence. **Science Education, 71**(1), 105-15.

Reports results of a study to determine whether differences existed between girls and boys regarding their concept structure interrelatedness competence (ConSIC) in the areas of physical science, life science, earth sciences, between sciences, within sciences and across all sciences by measuring ConSIC.

595. Harty, H., & Beall, D. (1984). Toward the development of a children's science curiosity measure. **Journal of Research in Science Teaching, 21**(4), 425-36.

Reports the development of a "Children's Science Curiosity Scale", composed of 30 Likert-like items which examine various curiosity factors in the context of science learning. Internal consistency, test-retest reliabilities, and validity of the instrument were investigated. Sex differences are discussed.

596. Harty, H., & Beall, D. (1984). Attitudes toward science of gifted and nongifted fifth graders. **Journal of Research in Science Teaching, 21**(5), 483-88.

Investigates whether differences existed between gifted and nongifted fifth graders and between sexes and related subgroups with respect to attitudes toward science. Although results indicate gifted students had more positive attitudes than nongifted students and boys had more positive attitudes than girls, findings are not statistically significant.

597. Harvey, T.J. (1985). Science in single-sex and mixed teaching groups. **Educational Research, 27**(3), 179-82.

Evidence of this study suggests that single-sex groups for science, whether in mixed schools or in single-sex schools, do not improve the attainment of girls in first-year science. Boys perform equally well on knowledge-based tests. On mechanical reasoning and evaluation of data tests, boys perform significantly better than girls.

598. Howe, A.C., & Shayer, M. (1981). Sex-related differences on a task of volume and density. **Journal of Research in Science Teaching, 18**(2), 169-75.

Reports results of a study of 10- and 11-year-old children on tasks involving volume and density. After classroom instruction that included opportunities for interaction with appropriate materials, both sexes performed at higher levels but differences remained.

599. Jacobowitz, T. (1983). Relationship of sex, achievement, and science self-concept to the science career preferences of black students. **Journal of Research in Science Teaching, 20**(7), 621-28.

Investigates relationships of mathematics/science achievement, science self-concept, and sex to science career preferences of black male and female junior high school students. Findings suggest that early adolescent science career preferences are related more to interests consonant with sex-role considerations than realistic assessment of mathematics/science achievement.

600. Jacobson, W.J., & Doran, R.L. (1985). How are our ninth graders doing? **Science Teacher, 52**(8), 24-27.

Compares the performance of ninth-grade students on 30 common test items given during the First (1970) and the Second (1983) International Science Study, including differences related to sex.

601. Jacobson, W.J., & Doran, R.L. (1985). The second international science study: U.S. results. **Phi Delta Kappan, 66**(6), 414-17.

Fifth and ninth graders in United States schools scored significantly higher in the Second International Science Study than did their counterparts in the first study conducted in 1970. Differences between the responses of males and females in 1983 are also noteworthy, especially at the 12th-grade level.

602. Jaus, H.H. (1981). Students tell teachers what they want from school. **Science and Children, 18**(6), 23.

Reports results of a questionnaire asking elementary school teachers and elementary school students what students want from schools. Findings indicate girls have interests equal to boys in science and science-oriented careers, and that teachers did not think their students were interested in science.

603. Kahle, J.B., et al (1985). An assessment of the impact of science experiences on the career choices of male and female biology students. **Journal of Research in Science Teaching, 22**(5), 385-94.

Examines data on students in biology classes where girls are encouraged in science, focusing on actual science experiences, masculine/feminine tasks, extracurricular science activities, feelings about science classes, research funding, and science career interest.

604. Karst, R.R. (1985). Energy opinions of southern, northern and academically prepared energy students in selected secondary schools. **Journal of Environmental Education, 16**(4), 17-24.

Examines effects of sex, grade level, region, and academic preparation of secondary school students on energy opinions. Assesses the responses of students on energy items related to the government, cars, and conservation. Results reveal significant regional and sex differences.

605. Kauchak, D., & Peterson, K. (1983). Differences in science students' view of ideal and actual role behavior according to success and gender. **Journal of Research in Science Teaching, 20**(6), 565-70.

A 20-item double-Q sort was used to measure differences in perceptions of grades 8, 10, and 12 students according to letter grades and sex. Differences in perception according to success are reported for both ideal and actual student behavior, while sex differences are not noted.

606. Kelly, A. (1988). Option choice for girls and boys. **Research in Science and Technological Education, 6**(1), 5-23.

Reports results of a study in which high school students were asked to identify factors influencing their school subject choice. Both sexes named the same influences. Support from parents, teachers, and friends are cited as strongest predictors of choice.

* Kelly, A. (1988). Sex stereotypes and school science: a three year follow-up. **Educational Studies.** (Cited as entry 728.)

607. Kuhn, D.J. (1980). A study of the attitudes of secondary school students toward energy related issues. **Southern Journal of Educational Research, 14**(1), 47-62.

Reports results of an 82-item questionnaire exploring such areas as energy conservation, pollution standards, specific energy types, and personal use of energy. Significant differences are noted between sexes in responses to certain items (e.g., need for energy conservation, potential for development of new resources), but sexes agreed on other items.

608. Lawrenz, F. (1983). Student knowledge of energy issues. **School Science and Mathematics, 83**(7), 587-95.

Assesses the current state of energy knowledge among students in order to identify areas in which future instruction would be most beneficial. Sex differences are discussed.

609. Lawrenz, F., & Dantchik, A. (1985). Attitudes toward energy among students in grades 4, 7 and high school. **School Science and Mathematics, 85**(3), 189-202.

Investigates developmental and/or sex components of energy attitudes using Kuhn's Energy Opinionnaire. Changes in student attitudes through grade levels are consistent with cognitive and affective development literature and sex differences are more pronounced in older students (with females having a more external world view than males).

610. Lawrenz, F., & Welch, W.W. (1983). Student perceptions of science classes taught by males and females. **Journal of Research in Science Teaching, 20**(7), 655-62.

Investigates whether students perceive science classroom environment in significantly different ways depending on their science teacher's sex. Reports differences (such as perceiving classes taught by males as more difficult), and possible relationships between these differences and changes in girl's preference for science.

* Lazarowitz, R. (1981). Correlations of junior high school students age, gender, and intelligence with ability in construct classification in biology. **Journal of Research in Science Teaching.** (Cited as entry 97.)

611. Lowery, L.F., et al. (1980). The Science Curriculum Improvement Study and student attitudes. **Journal of Research in Science Teaching, 17**(4), 327-35.

Investigates cumulative effects of SCIS on attitudes. Sex differences are discussed.

612. Ormerod, M.B. (1981). The social implications of science and science choices at 14+. **School Science Review, 63**(222), 164-67.

Suggesting a distinction between student attitudes toward science as a school subject (SUBATT) and toward the social implications of science (SOCATT), this study reports results of a study using various measures focusing on both. Sex differences are discussed.

613. Peterson, K. (1981). Ideal teacher behavior perceptions of science students: success, gender, course. **School Science and Mathematics, 81**(4), 315-21.

Significant differences in high school science students' perceptions of an ideal teacher are reported in this study. Sex differences are discussed.

614. Peterson, K., et al. (1980). Science students' role-specific self-concept: course, success, and gender. **Science Education, 64**(2), 169-74.

Explores relationships between role-specific self-concept, and demographic data, including type and level of course, science letter grade from previous semester, and gender of secondary school students.

* Pratt, D.L. (1985). Responsibility for student success/failure and observed verbal behavior among secondary science and mathematics teachers. **Journal of Research in Science Teaching.** (Cited as entry 574.)

615. Rakow, S.J. (1985). Prediction of the science inquiry skill of seventeen-year-olds: a test of the model of educational productivity. **Journal of Research in Science Teaching, 22**(4), 289-302.

Reports results of a study that (1) tested the effectiveness of the Model of Educational Productivity for predicting the inquiry skill of 17-year-olds; (2) investigated whether the prediction of inquiry differed for males and females; and (3) whether the prediction of inquiry skill differed for white and nonwhite students.

616. Rakow, S.J. (1984). What research says: what's happening in elementary science: a national assessment. **Science and Children, 22**(2), 39-40.

Examines science achievement, attitudes, sex differences, and racial differences among nine-year-olds. Compares these results to those from three previous National Assessment of Educational Progress studies.

617. Rand, D., & Gibb, L.H. (1989). A model program for gifted girls in science. **Journal for the Education of the Gifted, 12**(2), 142-55.

Reports the development of "Action Science" to increase gifted girls' involvement in science. For girls in grades 1-9, enjoyment of science activities, parental involvement, female role models, and hands-on investigations are emphasized.

618. Ridley, D.R., & Novak, J., & Alberta, D. (1983). Sex-related differences in high school science and mathematics enrollments: do they give males a critical headstart toward science and math-related careers? **Journal of Educational Research, 29**(4), 308-18.

Reports literature used to support hypothesis that enrollment in high school mathematics plays critical role in determining careers in science was not convincing. Concludes data on gender differences were too small to account for large gender differences in postsecondary careers.

619. Robinson, J.T. (1980). Student attitudes toward science courses in test schools using human sciences. **Journal of Research in Science Teaching, 17**(3), 231-41.

Compares effects of the Human Sciences Program (BSCS) and conventional programs on attitudes of eighth-grade students. Variables include course, gender and school (including teacher).

620. Saunders, W.L., & Shepardson, D. (1987). A comparison of concrete and formal science instruction upon science achievement and reasoning ability of sixth grade students. **Journal of Research in Science Teaching, 24**(1), 39-51.

Reports results of a study designed to examine the effect of concrete and formal instruction upon reasoning and science achievement of sixth grade students. Results indicate that the concrete instruction group had significantly higher levels of performance in science achievement and cognitive development and that males outperformed females.

621. Schoeneberger, M., & Russell, T. (1986). Elementary science as a little added frill: a report of two case studies. **Science Education, 70**(5), 519-38.

Reports results of case studies of science teaching at the elementary level, using two teachers as subjects. Addresses issues in elementary science teaching ranging from its importance at elementary level to gender differences in science instruction.

622. Sherris, J.D., & Kahle, J.B. (1984). The effects of instructional organization and locus of control orientation on meaningful learning in high school biology students. **Journal of Research in Science Teaching, 21**(1), 83-94.

Investigates effects on meaningful learning achievement of concept-related instructional organization and locus of control orientation of high school students. Results indicate that externally-oriented subjects exposed to the treatment generally retained more than those in a comparison group. Sex differences are discussed.

623. Shymansky, J. (1984). R&D centers. BSCS programs: just how effective were they? **American Biology Teacher, 46**(1), 54-57.

Examines Biological Sciences Curriculum Study programs showing how they compare to each other and other science programs and how various student groups perform. Student comparisons are made by sex, IQ, ability grouping, and socioeconomic status. Teacher background, school size and location are also examined. Summary and recommendations are included.

624. Silberstein, M., & Tamir, P. (1981). Factors which affect students' attitudes towards the use of living animals in learning biology. **Science Education, 65**(2), 119-30.

Identifies factors which affect students' attitudes toward the use of animals in research and in learning biology. Responses of students in grades 5, 7, 9, and 11 to questionnaires were analyzed by two-way analysis of variance by grade level and sex.

625. Simpson, R.D., & Oliver, J.S. (1985). Attitude toward science and achievement motivation profiles of male and female science students in grades six through ten. **Science Education, 69**(4), 511-26.

Reports results of a study to determine relationships between attitudes toward science, achievement motivation, and demographic variables over the school year and across grades (6-10) by sex.

626. Smail, B., & Kelly, A. (1984). Sex differences in science and technology among 11-year-old schoolchildren: I--cognitive. **Research in Science and Technological Education, 2**(1), 61-76.

Reports results of a study using three cognitive tests. Few sex differences among 11-year-old students are shown. Neither question style (multiple-choice or structured) nor content (masculine or feminine) had great effect on sex differences in performance. However, boys performed markedly better than girls on tests of spatial ability and mechanical reasoning.

627. Smith, W.S., & Erb, T.O. (1986). Effect of women science career role models on early adolescents' attitudes toward scientists and women in science. **Journal of Research in Science Teaching, 23**(8), 667-76.

Describes a study in which middle school/junior high school students were exposed to women science career role models as a part of their science instruction. Students' attitudes toward scientists and women in science were positively affected.

628. Spear, M.G. (1984). The biasing influence of pupil sex in a science marking exercise. **Research in Science and Technological Education, 2**(1), 55-60.

Examines secondary science teachers' sex bias in subjective evaluations of students' written work. Preliminary results reveal both male and female teachers tended to differentiate between work of boys and girls in similar ways.

629. Staver, J.R., & Halsted, D.A. (1985). The effects of reasoning, use of models, sex type, and their interactions on posttest achievement in chemical bonding after constant instruction. **Journal of Research in Science Teaching, 22**(5), 437-47.

Reports results of a study to determine the effects of reasoning, use of models during testing, and sex type on posttest achievement in chemical bonding under controlled instruction. Chemistry students' reasoning capabilities influenced performance; other variables were not significant. Sex differences are discussed.

630. Steinkamp, M.W., & Maehr, M.L. (1984). Gender differences in motivational orientations toward achievement in school science: a quantitative synthesis. **American Educational Research Journal, 21**(1), 39-59.

In a comprehensive review of the literature containing comparisons between boys and girls on motivation and/or achievement in science, findings were transformed into a common metric and analyzed. Reports sex differences in both motivation and achievement are smaller than is generally assumed, but occur.

631. Steinkamp, M.W., & Maehr, M.L. (1983). Affect, ability, and science achievement: a quantitative synthesis of correlational research. **Review of Educational Research, 53**(3), 369-96.

A quantitative synthesis of the results from 66 studies indicate that boys' and girls' science achievement is positively related to affect, but the relationship is weaker than expected. Findings indicate that science achievement correlates more strongly with cognitive abilities than with affect.

632. Subotnik, R.F. (1988). The motivation to experiment: a study of gifted adolescents' attitudes toward scientific research. **Journal**

for the Education of the Gifted, 11(3), 19-35.

Reports results of questionnaires completed by Westinghouse Science Talent Search winners who identified curiosity as their primary research impetus. Females reported more concern with social impacts of scientific research, less variability in self-image as scientists, and a greater tendency to credit hard work and dedication (versus intelligence/creativity) for success than males.

633. Taylor, J. (1979). Sexist bias in physics textbooks. **Physics Education, 14**(5), 277-80.

Information from a small survey of physics textbooks suggests girls are underrepresented in the texts and illustrations. Suggests if the pattern is apparent in all physics textbooks, this may be an indicator of why there is a paucity of females in physical sciences.

* Voekell, E.L., & Lobonc, S. (1981). Sex role stereotyping by high school females in science. **Journal of Research in Science Teaching.** (Cited as entry 68.)

634. Wandersee, J.H. (1986). Plants or animals--which do junior high school students prefer to study? **Journal of Research in Science Teaching, 23**(5), 415-26.

Reports results of a study to determine whether junior high school students prefer to study plants or animals and if their preferences are related to variables of grade level and/or sex. Findings show that, overall, students prefer animal study over plant study. Other findings (such as girls having a greater interest in biological topics than boys) are discussed.

635. Whyte, J. (1984). Observing sex stereotypes and interactions in the school lab and workshop. **Educational Review, 36**(1), 75-86.

Reports results of a study using techniques of classroom observation to increase teachers' awareness of the variable participation of boys and girls in science and craft lessons. Findings indicate that considerable effort may be needed to achieve the balanced participation by girls.

636. Williams, R.L., & Yore, L.D. (1985). Content, format, gender, and grade level differences in elementary students' ability to read science materials as measured by the cloze procedure. **Journal of Research in Science Teaching, 22**(1), 81-88.

Examines readability of elementary science textbooks regarding visual supplements (color, visuals, and page layout). Significant relationships are reported between cloze scores and both grade level and content. Also reports significant interaction between grade and sex in favor of older males.

637. Yager, R.E., et al. (1988). Features which separate least effective from most effective science teachers. **Journal of Research in Science Teaching, 25**(3), 165-77.

Reports results of a study which asked science supervisors to identify their most effective and least effective teachers. Differences were found regarding gender, quantity of National Science Foundation workshop experiences, and certain elected in-service experiences.

638. Zerega, M.E., et al. (1986). Late adolescent sex differences in science learning. **Science Education, 70**(4), 447-60.

Explores sex differences in science achievement and examines the possible environmental determinants of these differences. Results show males scoring significantly higher on science achievement and motivation. Findings also show males perceived their classroom environment more positively than females.

Self-Esteem | Self-Concept | Self-Awareness

639. Abbott, A.A. (1981). Factors related to third grade achievement: self-perception, classroom composition, sex and race. **Contemporary Educational Psychology, 6**(2), 167-79.

Examines race, sex, IQ, self-perception, and student's perceptions of their teacher's perceptions as sources of variance in academic achievement. Findings show self-perceptions account for more variance in academic achievement for students who are of the same sex and race as the teacher than for those who are not.

640. Barnes, M.E., & Farrier, S.C. (1985). A longitudinal study of the self-concept of low-income youth. **Adolescence, 20**(77), 199-205.

Reports results of interviews with elementary school children in 1969 and follow-up interviews in 1978 to determine the stability of self-concept over a decade. Sex, race, and residence are used as independent variables.

641. Bell, L.A. (1989). Something's wrong here and it's not me: challenging the dilemmas that block girls' success. **Journal for the Education of the Gifted, 12**(2), 118-130.

Explores 6 core dilemmas that block girls' success in school through discussions with 4th-6th graders. Core dilemmas are smart vs. social, silence vs. bragging, failure vs. perfection, "beauty" vs. marginality, passive vs. aggressive, and conforming vs. being punished. Examples illustrate how girls can learn to externalize situational conflict and create options that express their own values and preferences.

642. Block, J.H. (1981). The difference between boys and girls: how gender roles are shaped. **Principal, 60**(5), 41-45.

Reports results of a longitudinal study of the ego and cognitive development of boys and girls. Findings show that sex-different socialization practices cause the two sexes to create different premises about the world, develop different competencies, and use different cognitive structures to deal with new experience.

643. Brinthaup, T.M., & Lipka, R.P. (1985). Developmental differences in self-concept and self-esteem among kindergarten through twelfth grade students. **Child Study Journal, 15**(3), 207-21.

Reports results of a study using responses by kindergarten through twelfth-graders to a request, "Tell me about yourself." Self-concept content, self-esteem judgments, and other criteria were analyzed. Sex differences are discussed.

644. Brown, D., et al. (1984). Locus of control, sex role orientation, and self-concept in black and white third- and sixth- grade male and female leaders in a rural community. **Developmental Psychology, 20**(4), 717-21.

Reports results of a study that show white leaders exhibited more internal control and attributed good outcomes to personal attributes more often than did black leaders. Self-concept data and sex-role orientation data were not helpful in interpreting findings.

645. Brown, D., et al. (1983). Self-estimate ability in black and white 8th-, 10th-, and 12th-grade males and females. **Vocational Guidance Quarterly, 32**(1), 21-28.

Explores the ability of students in grades 8, 10, and 12, to estimate their scores on psychometric instruments measuring self-awareness. No sex or age differences were found, but black students are reported as less accurate in their self-assessments than whites.

646. Burdett, K., & Jensen, L.C. (1983). The self-concept and aggressive behavior among elementary school children from two socioeconomic areas and two grade levels. **Psychology in the Schools, 20**(3), 370-75.

Investigates the relationship between self-concept and aggressive behavior in third- and sixth-grade students. Analysis of variance reveals significantly larger aggressiveness scores among low self-concept children. Girls, while less aggressive than boys, are reported as more aggressive by age while boys are reported as less aggressive. No socioeconomic influences were found.

647. Byrne, B.M. (1988). Measuring adolescent self-concept: factorial validity and equivalency of the SDQ III across gender. **Multivariate Behavioral Research, 23**(3), 361-375.

Reports the use of exploratory (EFA) and confirmatory (CFA) factor analyses to investigate the factorial validity of the Self Description Questionnaire III (SDQ III) subscales measuring general, school, English, and mathematics self-concepts for male and female students, grades 11 and 12.

648. Calsyn, R.J., & Prost, B. (1983). Evaluation of an affective education curriculum: sex and treatment effects. **The Journal of Humanistic Education and Development, 22**(2), 58-69.

Evaluates the success of an affective education curriculum for fifth-grade students. Results indicate the eight-week program had a positive impact on students' self-esteem. Teacher ratings suggest that the program also had a positive effect on students' peer relationships. Treatment appears to have made more difference for males.

649. Calsyn, R.J., et al. (1984). Are affective education programs more effective with girls than with boys? **Elementary School Guidance and Counseling, 19**(2), 132-40.

Examines the influence of an affective education program on self-esteem in sixth- and seventh-grade students. Results of pretest, posttest, and a two-month follow-up suggest girls benefited more than boys from the treatment.

650. Cate, R., & Sugawara, A. (1986). Sex role orientation and dimensions of self-esteem among middle adolescents. **Sex Roles: A Journal of Research, 15**(3-4), 145-58.

Examines the relationships between sex role orientation and self-esteem among adolescents, using Harter's (1982) Perceived Competence Scale for Children (PCSC) and the Personal Attributes Questionnaire Short Form (PAQ). Results support the masculinity model of psychological well-being and suggest that this model is applicable to both global and specific dimensions.

651. Culver, S.M., & Burge, P.L. (1985). Self-concept of students in vocational programs nontraditional for their sex. **Journal of Vocational Education Research, 10**(2), 1-9.

Reports results of a study examining the differences in self-concept of students grouped according to their sex and the predominance of one sex in their vocational programs. Males, on the whole, reported more positive self-concepts than females.

652. Douglas, J., & Rice, K.M. (1979). Sex differences in children's anxiety and defensiveness measures. **Developmental Psychology, 15**(2), 223-24.

Investigates whether girls' higher scores on self-report measures of anxiety in elementary school is a reflection of sex differences in attitudes toward the admission of anxiety.

653. Freeman, S.J.M., & Giebink, J.W. (1979). Moral judgment as a function of age, sex, and stimulus. **Journal of**

Psychology, 113(3), 43-47.

Provides data in support of Lawrence Kohlberg's moral development theory. Shows comparable moral judgments for boys and girls at ages 11 and 17, but higher moral reasoning in 14-year-old girls than in their male peers.

654. Frieze, I.H., & Snyder, H.N. (1980). Children's beliefs about the causes of success and failure in school settings. **Journal of Educational Psychology, 72**(2), 186-96.

Reports results of interviewing Catholic elementary school children to determine what they saw as probable causes for success or failure in four situations: a school testing situation, an art project, playing football, and catching frogs. Causal explanations were found to differ across the four situations. Sex differences are discussed.

* Gaa, J.P., et al. (1981). Domain-specific locus of control orientations of Anglo, black, and Chicano adolescents. **Journal of Psychology.** (Cited as entry 157.)

655. Gade, E., & Peterson, L. (1980). A comparison of working and nonworking high school students on school performance, socioeconomic status, and self-esteem. **Vocational Guidance Quarterly, 29**(1), 65-69.

Reports results of a study of working high school students finding them similar on school achievement, extracurricular involvement, and self-esteem. Girls employed were more often from families of upper socioeconomic levels than nonemployed girls.

656. Gitelson, I.B., et al. (1982). Adolescents' expectancies of success, self-evaluations, and attributions about performance on spatial and verbal tasks. **Sex Roles: A Journal of Research, 8**(4), 411-19.

Reports results of a study of the expectancies of success, evaluations of performance, and achievement-related attributions about tasks that typically show sex differences. Results suggest generalized, rather than task specific, sex differences in achievement expectancies, evaluations, and attributions.

657. Gold, A.R., et al. (1980). Developmental changes in self-perceptions of intelligence and self-confidence. **Psychology of Women Quarterly, 5**(2), 231-39.

Examines sex differences in self-perceptions of intelligence and self-confidence. In third grade, perceptions of intelligence favored females; by fifth grade, males were favored. Differences persisted into eighth grade. Sex differences could not be explained by internalizing sex-stereotypes.

* Handley, H.M., & Morse, L.W. (1984). Two-year study relating adolescents' self-concept and gender role perceptions to achievement and attitudes toward science. **Journal of Research in Science Teaching.** (Cited as entry 593.)

658. Hauck, W.E., et al. (1986). Shyness, group dependence and self-concept: attributes of the imaginary audience. **Adolescence, 21**(83), 529-34.

Examines sensitivity to an imaginary audience, shyness, group dependence, and self-concept in adolescents. Reports that ninth-graders were higher in group dependence and were more sensitive to an imaginary audience than either seventh or eleventh graders. Subjects highly sensitive to imaginary audiences projected shyness, which increased with age, and low self-concepts. Sex differences are discussed.

659. Hughes, C.M., et al. (1985). Sex role attitudes and career choices: the role of children's self-esteem. **Elementary School Guidance and Counseling, 20**(1), 57-66.

Examines relationships between self-esteem, career attitudes, and career choice among elementary school children. Results indicate that for girls the relationship between self-esteem and nontraditional attitudes is reliably established as early as the primary years in school. Conversely, boys with high self-esteem possess more traditional notions concerning sex roles in the workplace.

* Husak, W.S., & Magill, R.A. (1979). Correlations among perceptual-motor ability, self-concept and reading achievement in early elementary grades. **Perceptual and Motor Skills.** (Cited as entry 279.)

660. Ilardi, B.C., & Bridges, L.J. (1988). Gender differences in self-esteem processes as rated by teachers and students. **Sex Roles: A Journal of Research, 18**(5-6), 333-42.

Reports results of a study of grade 4 and 6 children showing girls are less likely than boys to underrate their abilities assessed by test scores, but more likely to underrate teacher assessments of competence. Teachers rate boys who underrate themselves lower than they do boys who overrate themselves, but do the reverse for girls.

661. Isbitsky, J.R., & White, D.R. (1981). Externality and locus of control in obese children. **Journal of Psychology, 107**(2), 163-72.

Reports results of a study in which significant sex differences indicate that boys generally ate more than girls and held more internal locus of control expectancies.

662. Jaquish, G.A., & Savin-Williams, R.C. (1981). Biological and ecological factors in the expression of adolescent self-esteem. **Journal of Youth and Adolescence, 10**(6), 473-85.

Reports results of a longitudinal study of the relationship between self-esteem and pubertal maturation, based on data gathered in the first two years of the study. Sex differences are discussed.

* Kamalanabhan, T.J. (1988). Efficacy of a behavioral program for personality change and improvement in academic

performance of school students. **Journal of Psychological Research.** (Cited as entry 14.)

663. Kanoy, R.C., III, et al. (1980). Locus of control and self-concept in achieving and underachieving bright elementary students. **Psychology in the Schools, 17**(1), 395-99.

Reports results showing achievers had significantly higher self-concepts than underachievers on the Intellectual and School Status subscale. Achievers had significantly higher internal locus of control scores than underachievers for the Intellectual Achievement Responsibility Questionnaire's total score and positive score. No sex differences were revealed.

664. Kelemen, V.P. Jr. (1980). Achievement and affiliation: a motivational perspective of sex differences. **Social Behavior and Personality, 8**(1), 1-11.

Reports results of a study showing that for both males and females, age and education are important factors in the determination of achievement behavior. While results fail to resolve the achievement versus affiliation argument, they nevertheless support the lessening importance of sex-role stereotyping.

665. Lempers, J.D., et al. (1989). Economic hardship, parenting, and distress in adolescence. **Child Development, 60**(1), 25-40.

Investigates relationship between family economic hardship and adolescent distress among students in grades 9-12. Hardship effects are reported as varying according to type of distress. Hardship had direct and indirect effects on depression-loneliness factor and indirect effect on the delinquency-drug use factor. Sex differences are discussed.

666. Lerner, R.M., et al. (1981). Sex differences in self-concept and self-esteem of late adolescents: a time-lag analysis. **Sex-Roles: A Journal of Research, 7**(7), 709-22.

Reports results of a study of presence of historical change in the self-concept and self-esteem of male and female late adolescents.

667. Leroux, J.A. (1988). Voices from the classroom: academic and social self-concepts of gifted adolescents. **Journal for the Education of the Gifted, 11**(3), 3-18.

Reports results of questionnaires and interviews completed by gifted adolescents. Findings show both sexes highly sensitive to societal pressures. Females accepted their body image, social image, and inner emotions better than males who perceived themselves as having poorer peer relationships and less leadership potential. Case studies illustrate representative sex differences.

668. Louie, S., et al. (1986). Locus of control among computer-using school children: a report of a pilot study. **Journal of Educational Technology Systems, 14**(2), 101-18.

Describes a study in which high socioeconomic status elementary and secondary children were exposed to Logo and Bank Street Writer at a computer camp. After exposure, children 12 and under minimally shifted toward an internal locus of control as measured by the Nowicki-Strickland Locus of Control Scale for Children.

669. Mark, E.W., & Alper, T.G. (1980). Sex differences in intimacy motivation. **Psychology of Women Quarterly, 5**(2), 164-69.

Use of a projective cue with a sample of high school students indicated highly significant sex differences in Intimacy Imagery. Males who showed a stereotypically masculine orientation in their projective responses to two cues were less likely than other males to write stories containing Intimacy Imagery.

670. Marsh, H.W., et al. (1984). Self-description questionnaire: age and sex effects in the structure and level of self-concept for preadolescent children. **Journal of Educational Psychology, 76**(5), 940-56.

Reports results of a study in which factor analyses of responses to the self-description questionnaire (SDQ) by children in grades two to five, clearly identified the seven SDQ factors. Findings show correlations were consistent with Shavelson's model. Results also suggest that these factors become more distinct with age. Sex differences are reported.

671. Martin, S., & Cowles, M. (1983). Locus of control among children in various educational environments. **Perceptual and Motor Skills, 56**(3), 831-34.

Reports results of administering the Stephens-Delys Reinforcement Contingency Interview to subjects, 6.5 years to 7.5 years, who were enrolled in "traditional" or "open" educational programs. Scores are categorized by sex, race, economic level and educational program, and treated by analysis of variance.

672. Massad, C.M. (1981). Sex role identity and adjustment during adolescence. **Child Development, 52**(4), 1290-98.

Examines the relationship between sex role identity and two measures of adjustment--self-acceptance and peer acceptance--among adolescents. Sex differences are reported regarding factors positively associated with self-acceptance. Findings suggest that a model of sex role differentiation during adolescence must recognize differential pressures on male and female adolescents to conform.

673. Mendelson, B.K., & White, D.R. (1985). Development of self-esteem in overweight youngsters. **Developmental Psychology, 21**(1), 90-96.

Examines development of self-body-esteem and relation between self-esteem and body-esteem in overweight and normal weight boys and girls in three age groups.
Results are interpreted by age differences in subjects and possible social influences in development of self-esteem in overweight youngsters.

674. Mills, R.S.L., & Grusec, J.E. (1989). Cognitive, affective, and

behavioral consequences of praising altruism. **Merrill-Palmer Quarterly, 35**(3), 299-326.

Reports results of studies investigating effects of dispositional praise on internalized sharing and self-perception of 8 and 9 year-old children. Sex differences are discussed.

675. Newman, R.S., & Wick, P.L. (1987). Effect of age, skill, and performance feedback on children's judgments of confidence. **Journal of Educational Psychology, 79**(2), 115-19.

Examines children's judgments of confidence following performance on a cognitive task as a function of age and skill and the presence or absence of feedback. Results suggest that domain-specific knowledge, in conjunction with feedback, may help young children compensate for developmental factors associated with an unrealistically high degree of confidence. Sex differences are discussed.

676. Ollendick, D.G. (1979). Locus of control and anxiety as mediating variables of locus of conflict in disadvantaged youth. **Journal of Psychology, 101,** 23-25.

Reports results of a study using the hypothesis that external locus of control scores correlate significantly with locus of conflict scores. Findings show correlation although this varied for both sex and for type of behavior problems exhibited.

677. Orton, G.L. (1982). A comparative study of children's worries. **Journal of Psychology, 110**(2), 153-62.

In the late thirties Pinter and Lev discovered that fifth and sixth graders in New York City worried most about family and school items, with the greatest single worry being "failing a test." The present study was designed to replicate that work and to determine whether changing social, economic, and political conditions have affected the worries of children. Sex differences are discussed.

678. Osborne, W.L., & LeGette, H.R. (1982). Sex, race, grade level, and social class differences in self-concept. **Measurement and Evaluation in Guidance, 14**(4), 195-201.

Reports results of a study obtaining global self-concept scores as well as perceptions of various dimensions of self for students of grades 7, 9, and 11. Data indicate significant sex, race, grade level, and social class differences.

679. Ottenbacher, K. (1981). An investigation of self-concept and body image in the mentally retarded. **Journal of Clinical Psychology, 37**(2), 415-18.

Explores the relationship of self-drawings to self-concept in mentally retarded youths. Overall self-drawing score, size of self-drawing, age and sex shared significant variance with self-concept scores.

680. Payne, B.D., & Payne, D.A. (1989). Sex, race, and grade differences in the locus of control orientations of at-risk elementary students. **Psychology in the Schools, 26**(1), 84-88.

Investigates relationship between academic achievement and locus of control among 643 elementary school students. Reports significant effect for condition (at-risk versus not-at-risk), with at-risk students being more externally oriented. Shows significant effect for grade, trend being for grade (age) to be positively related to internality. No main effects for gender or race are shown.

* Peeler, E., & Rimmer, S.M. (1981). The assertiveness scale for children. **Elementary School Guidance and Counseling.** (Cited as entry 474.)

681. Pellegrini, D.S. (1985). Social cognition and competence in middle childhood. **Child Development, 56**(1), 153-64.

Evaluates fourth-to seventh-grade children on two aspects of social cognition: interpersonal understanding and means-ends problem-solving ability. Relates the two variables to sex, age, IQ, social class, and multiple dimensions of competence. Both variables significantly correlate with IQ while interpersonal understanding also correlated with age and social class.

682. Pillen, B.L., et al. (1988). The effects of gender on the transition of transfer students into a new school. **Psychology in the Schools, 25**(2), 187-94.

Reports results of administering a peer-tutoring program using computer-assisted instruction to help first through fourth graders enter a new school. Findings show tutored girls increased positive self-perceptions as result of program, whereas boys declined in positive self-perceptions, but exhibited gains in reading scores.

683. Pomerantz, S.C. (1979). Sex differences in the relative importance of self-esteem, physical self-satisfaction, and identity in predicting adolescent satisfaction. **Journal of Youth and Adolescence, 8**(1), 51-61.

Investigates interrelationships of physical self-satisfaction, self-esteem, and identity, and their ability to predict satisfaction with an individual's social milieu. Prediction patterns yield no differences between grades 8, 10, and 12. Findings show self-esteem as the best predictor for males and identity and physical self-satisfaction for females.

684. Prawat, R.S., et al. (1979). Affective development in children, grades 3 through 12. **Journal of Genetic Psychology, 135**(1), 37-50.

Assesses the affective development of children in grades 3 through 12 through use of instruments measuring self-esteem, locus of control and achievement motivation. Sex differences are discussed.

685. Prawat, R.S., et al. (1979). Longitudinal study of attitude

development in pre-, early, and later adolescent samples. **Journal of Educational Psychology, 71**(3), 363-69.

Changes in attitude were examined over a one-year period in pre-, early, and later adolescent samples. Self-esteem, locus of control, and achievement motivation were examined. The amount of attitudinal change evidenced by subjects at each age level varied with the kind of attitude being assessed. Sex differences are discussed.

686. Reynolds, C.R., et al. (1980). Preliminary norms and technical data for use of the Revised-Children's Manifest Anxiety Scale with kindergarten children. **Psychology in the Schools, 17**(2), 163-67.

Reports results of a study showing that contrary to findings with older children, no sex differences occurred in anxiety scale scorings.

687. Reynolds, W.M. (1980). Self-esteem and classroom behavior in elementary school children. **Psychology in the Schools, 17**(2), 273-77.

Reports results of a study recommending that since there is a moderately positive correlation between behavior and self-esteem, teachers who desire to modify classroom behavior of students should follow procedure that is congruent with enhancing and maintaining students' self-attitude. Sex differences are discussed.

688. Richman, C.L., et al. (1984). The relationship between self-esteem and maladaptive behaviors in high school students. **Social Behavior and Personality, 12**(2), 177-85.

Reports general and area specific self-esteem scores of high school students to be inversely related to indices of maladaptive behavior. The specific maladaptive behaviors associated with self-esteem varied as a function of gender and social class.

689. Ryckman, D.B., & Peckham, P.D. (1987). Gender differences

in attributions for success and failure situations across subject areas. **Journal of Educational Research, 81**(2), 120-25.

Reports results of administering the Survey of Achievement Responsibility (SOAR) to girls and boys in grades 4 through 12 to determine gender differences in attributions of success and failure across subject areas.

690. Silvern, L.E., & Katz, P.A. (1986). Gender roles and adjustment in elementary-school children: a multidimensional approach. **Sex Roles: A Journal of Research, 14**(3-4), 181- 202.

Examines the relations between fourth- through sixth-grade students' school adjustment and the extent to which their self concepts conform to stereotypic gender roles. Among boys, more stereotypic self-concepts are associated with high levels of externalizing conduct disorders. Among girls, stereotypy was associated with high levels of internalizing.

691. Simmons, R.G., et al. (1979). Entry into early adolescence: the impact of school structure, puberty, and early dating on self-esteem. **American Sociological Review, 44**(6), 948-67.

Reports findings that indicate seventh-grade white adolescent girls who enter a new junior high school are at a disadvantage in self-esteem when compared to boys, in general, and to girls who do not have to change schools.

* Smith, T.L. (1988). Self-concept and teacher expectation of academic achievement in elementary school children. **Journal of Instructional Psychology.** (Cited as entry 30.)

692. Stewart, C.G., & Lewis, W.A. (1986). Effects of assertiveness training on the self-esteem of black high school students. **Journal of Counseling & Development, 64**(10), 638-41.

Effects of assertiveness training on assertive behaviors and self-esteem were investigated among black high school students. Results show a significant difference between scores of males and females on the written assertiveness measure. Scores of females accounted for all of the change, whereas scores of males actually dropped somewhat.

693. Stipek, D.J., et al. (1981). OPTI: a measure of children's optimism. **Educational and Psychological Measurement, 41**(1), 131-43.

Reports results of a test of validity and reliability of the Optimism-Pessimism Test Instrument (OPTI). Moderate, but significant, correlations are reported between OPTI and attitude toward school, self-concept, delay of gratification, and locus of control. Sex differences are discussed.

694. Street, S. (1981). Social self concept in high school students. **School Counselor, 28**(5), 315-23.

Reports results of a study of the development of high school students' self-social relationships indicating need for a concentrated program on personal growth and development in tenth grade when individual identities are forming. Findings show high school students scored highest on self-complexity and self-centrality tests. Developmental trends for sex are also indicated.

695. Styer, S. (1988). Sex equity: a moral development approach. **Social Education, 52**(3), 173-75.

Presents a moral development approach to achieving sex equity. Study used discussion of carefully developed Kohlberg-type moral dilemmas relating to sex equity to elicit moral judgments from children at a number of developmental stages.

* Subotnik, R.F. (1988). The motivation to experiment: a study of gifted adolescents' attitudes toward scientific research. **Journal for the Education of the Gifted.** (Cited as entry 632.)

696. Swager, R.G. (1981). Self-disclosure and the school guidance counselor. **School Counselor, 29**(1), 28-33.

Provides an overview of recent research on self-disclosure and describes how various research findings are applicable to school counseling. Outlines specific questions important for counselors relating to age and sex differences.

* Tinsley, H.E., et al. (1984). The effects of values clarification exercises on the value structure of junior high school students. **Vocational Guidance Quarterly.** (Cited as entry 66.)

697. Vaughan, S.L., et al. (1981). Children's monetary evaluations of body parts as a function of sex, race, and school grade. **Journal of Psychology, 107**(2), 203-08.

Reports results of a study in which male children valued their bodies more than females. Black children placed higher values on their bodies than white children.

698. Wagenaar, T.C. (1981). High school seniors' views of themselves and their schools: a trend analysis. **Phi Delta Kappan, 63**(1), 29-32.

Compares two major studies on high school seniors' views of themselves and their schools revealing how their attitudes changed during the 1970s. Sex differences are discussed.

699. Wass, H., et al. (1989). Adolescents' interest in and views of destructive themes in rock music. **Omega: Journal of Death and Dying, 19**(3), 177-86.

Reports results of a survey of adolescents concerning rock music preferences and views on homicide, satanism, and suicide (HSS) themes. Nine percent of middle school students, 17 percent of rural and 24 percent of urban high school students are shown as HSS rock fans. Reports three-fourths of fans as male, and majority as white. Many students expressed concerns about destructive lyrics in rock music.

700. Wolf, T.M., et al. (1982). Factor analytic study of the children's Nowicki-Strickland Locus of Control Scale. **Educational and Psychological Measurement, 42**(1), 333-37.

Reports results of a factor analysis of the Children's Nowicki-Strickland Locus of Control Scale conducted with a biracial sample of children over a wide age range. Three factors (personal control and helplessness, achievement and friendship, and luck) show sufficient item loadings to be interpretable. Sex differences are discussed.

701. Wong, B.Y.L., & Wong, R. (1980). Role-taking skills in normal achieving and learning disabled children. **Learning Disability Quarterly, 3**(2), 11-18.

Reports results of a study showing LD children as much less able to adopt an alternative viewpoint than their normal counterparts. Moreover, within the group of LD children, females are shown as substantially more egocentric than males.

Sex Roles | Socialization | Stereotyping

* Ahlgren, A., & Johnson, D.W. (1979). Sex differences in cooperative and competitive attitudes from the 2nd through the 12th grades. **Developmental Psychology.** (Cited as entry 458.)

* Albert, A.A., & Porter, J.R. (1986). Children's gender roles stereotypes: a comparison of the United States and South Africa. **Journal of Cross-Cultural Psychology.** (Cited as entry 150.)

702. Bardwell, J.R., et al. (1986). Relationship of parental education, race, and gender to sex role stereotyping in five-year-old kindergartners. **Sex Roles: A Journal of Research, 15**(5-6), 275-81.

Reports results of a study of sex-role stereotyping in five-year-olds in which white children gave more stereotyped responses than did black children. Stereotyping increased as parent educational level increased. Latter trend was not evidenced in black children, and no significant differences in stereotyping were noted between the sexes.

* Barnhart, R.S. (1983). Children's sex-typed views of traditional occupational roles. **School Counselor.** (Cited as entry 39.)

703. Baumrind, D. (1982). Are androgynous individuals more effective persons and parents? **Child Development, 53**(1), 44-75.

Examines claims that androgynes, by comparison with sex-typed individuals, are more effective persons and parents, by using multifaceted observational and interview data from the family socialization and developmental competence project.

704. Bearison, D.J. (1979). Sex-linked patterns of socialization. **Sex Roles: A Journal of Research, 5**(1), 11-18.

Explores how mothers socialize their daughters in ways systematically different from how they socialize their sons. Also examines whether these differences are related, in turn, to systematically different ways in which fathers socialize their sons and daughters.

* Bem, S.L. (1981). Gender schema theory: a cognitive account of sex typing. **Psychological Review.** (Cited as entry 75.)

705. Benz, C.R., et al. (1981). Sex role expectations of classroom teachers, grades 1-12. **American Educational Research Journal, 18**(3), 289-302.

Assesses the effect of variables of student sex, grade level, and student achievement on teacher sex role expectations. Of the four variables, student achievement is shown as a highly significant predictor. A negative relationship is shown between the feminine sex role and high achievement.

* Blakemore, J.E.O., et al. (1979). Sex-appropriate toy preference and the ability to conceptualize toys as sex-role related. **Developmental Psychology.** (Cited as entry 789.)

706. Blanck, P.D., et al. (1984). The effects of verbal reinforcement on intrinsic motivation for sex-linked tasks. **Sex Roles: A Journal of Research, 10**(5-6), 369-86.

Results of two experiments show that (1) verbal praise increased males' and females' intrinsic motivation on masculine and feminine tasks, and intrinsic motivation was higher for sex-appropriate than sex-inappropriate tasks; and (2) praise enhanced traditional females' intrinsic motivation even on a task that in earlier research showed striking differences.

707. Bridges, J.S., & Del Ciampo, J. (1981). Children's perceptions of the competence of boys and girls. **Perceptual and Motor Skills, 52**(2), 503-06.

Reports results of a study in which upper middle-class first- and third-graders indicated how well they thought a boy or girl was performing activities classified as masculine, feminine, or neutral. Subjects of both sexes tended to assign more competence to performance of sex-appropriate roles. On neutral activities, boys tended to devalue girls' competence.

708. Brounstein, P.J., et al. (1988). The expectations and motivations of gifted students in a residential academic program: a study of individual differences. **Journal for the Education of the Gifted, 11**(3), 36-52.

Reports results of a survey of extremely gifted adolescents enrolled in the Talent Identification Program. Findings suggest tendency among gifted females to be more social and gregarious and better balanced between social and achievement interests than males warrants further investigation.

709. Cann, A., & Palmer, S. (1986). Children's assumptions about the generalization of sex-typed abilities. **Sex Roles: A Journal of Research, 15**(9-10), 551-58.

A sample of children (grades 2-3) was provided with information about the abilities of two children at a specific activity and asked to predict their abilities at a second related activity. The respondents' sex stereotypes interfered with their capacity to make logical inferences about the stimulus children's abilities at the second activity.

710. Cann, A., & Haight, J.M. (1983). Children's perceptions of relative competence in sex-typed occupations. **Sex Roles: A Journal of Research, 9**(7), 767-73.

Children were asked to choose either a male or female doll in response to a question as to which would be better at an occupation. Results show children of all ages have clear sex-typed expectations concerning occupational competence, and with increasing age there is an increasing adherence to these stereotypes.

711. Canter, R.J., & Ageton, S.S. (1984). The epidemiology of adolescent sex-role attitudes. **Sex Roles: A Journal of Research, 11**(7-8), 657-76.

Describes a study which examined the epidemiology of sex-role attitudes among a national probability sample of American adolescents. Reports indicate that more traditional sex-role attitudes are held by male, lower-class, and minority respondents. Assesses the impact of sex-role attitudes on conventional and delinquent behaviors and values.

* Cate, R., & Sugawara, A. (1986). Sex role orientation and dimensions of self-esteem among middle adolescents. **Sex Roles: A Journal of Research.** (Cited as entry 650.)

712. Colangelo, N., & Parker, M. (1981). Value differences among gifted adolescents. **Counseling and Values, 26**(1), 35-41.

Gifted high school students responded to a values survey consisting of two sets of 18 values: instrumental values and terminal values. Results show no differences by sex in value patterns, academic performance, and self-concept. Suggests that sex-role stereotyped expectations still persist for the gifted in school and society.

713. DiMartino, E.C. (1989). The relationship between age, sex and the language of social regulation. **Child Study Journal, 19**(1), 1-28.

Investigates relationship between age and sex and ability to differentiate social regulatory transactions among boys and girls and adult males and females. Reports significant differences in social regulatory understanding due to age and sex.

714. Dweck, C.S., et al. (1980). Sex differences in learned helplessness: IV: an experimental and naturalistic study of failure generalization and its mediators. **Journal of Personality and Social Psychology, 38**(3), 441-52.

Reports results of two experiments conducted to examine the role of sex differences among elementary school students in learned helplessness in the generalization of failure experience.

715. Emmerich, W., & Shepard, K. (1984). Cognitive factors in the development of sex-typed preferences. **Sex Roles: A Journal of Research, 11**(11-12), 997-1007.

Assesses sex-typed preferences and gender constancy at ages four through eight on a cross section of urban children. Findings verify sex-stereotyped preferences are highly developed among young children, and that, by age five, most children accurately attribute sex-stereotyped preferences to peers of the opposite sex.

716. Engel, R.E. (1981). Is unequal treatment of females diminishing in children's picture books? **Reading Teacher, 34**(6), 647-52.

Reveals that more male than female characters appear in recent Caldecott Medal and Honor books.

717. Eron, L.D. (1980). Prescription for reduction of aggression. **American Psychologist, 35**(3), 244-52.

Reviews the results of a longitudinal study on socialization and child aggression. Proposes boys be exposed to the same training that girls have traditionally received, and that they be encouraged to develop similar socially positive, nurturant, and sensitive qualities antithetical to aggressive behavior.

718. Etaugh, C., et al. (1984). Development of sex biases in children: 40 years later. **Sex Roles: A Journal of Research, 10**(11-12), 913-24.

On sex bias measures, children (grades 2-10) assigned more desirable traits to their own sex and more undesirable traits to the opposite sex. Both sexes became less positive toward their own sex with increasing age. Availability of "both sexes" option decreased stereotyping, especially in girls.

719. Fist, W.R. (1985). Responses to "Newtral" pronoun presentations and the development of sex-biased responding. **Developmental Psychology, 21**(3), 481-85.

Examines whether kindergarten and first-grade children give sex-biased responses if reinforced and/or triggered by oral language, specifically pronouns. Results support the pronominal dominance theory of pronoun functioning for young children. Results also suggest that boys but not girls use a self-imaging response to neutral presentations.

720. Freire, E., et al. (1980). Temporal span, delay of gratification, and children's socioeconomic status. **Journal of Genetic Psychology, 137**(2), 247-55.

Reports results of a study to assess time perspective, delay of gratification and future self-image. All measures were found to be significantly and highly related to socioeconomic status. Sex differences are discussed.

721. Goetz, J.P. (1981). Children's sex-role knowledge and behavior: an ethnographic study of first graders in the rural south. **Theory and Research in Social Education, 8**(4), 1-13.

Examines the extent to which two classrooms of rural southern first graders shared common sex-role beliefs within an institutional setting that emphasized conflicting (traditional and egalitarian) gender-specific expectations. Boys and girls drew from the total range of masculine, feminine, and neutral behaviors with few restrictions by gender identity.

722. Hanes, B., et al. (1979). Sex role perceptions during adolescence. **Journal of Educational Psychology, 71**(6), 850-55.

Reports results of a study of male and female responses to self-esteem and locus of control instruments. Findings show both sexes perceived themselves as more internally controlled than the opposite sex. Subjects also credited males as higher in self-esteem when responding as they thought a member of the opposite sex would respond.

723. Hensen, S.L., & Darling, C.A. (1985). Attitudes of adolescents toward division of labor in the home. **Adolescence, 20**(77), 61-72.

Asks whether adolescents are becoming more egalitarian in their approach to sex roles. Examines adolescents' attitudes toward household tasks based on gender and maternal employment. Findings indicate adolescents' attitudes were still somewhat traditional.

724. Horstman, A.M., & Bornstein, P.H. (1985). Children's judgments of socially skilled versus socially deficient female peers. **Child and Family Behavior Therapy, 7**(1), 51-64.

Studies the relationship between third graders' social skill behaviors and peer judgments. Children assessing videotaped vignettes in which female peers exhibited different social skills and deficits responded more favorably to socially skilled girls. Furthermore, gender apparently influenced children's sociometric and attractiveness ratings of female peers, but not social skill ratings.

* Hughes, C.M., et al. (1985). Sex role attitudes and career choices: the role of children's self-esteem. **Elementary School guidance and Counseling.** (Cited as entry 659.)

725. Huston, A.C. (1984). Children's comprehension of televised formal features with masculine and feminine connotations. **Developmental Psychology, 20**(4), 707-16.

Children from grades one through six judged commercially produced advertisements, specially produced "pseudocommercials", and verbal descriptions as better suited to advertise a feminine or masculine sex-typed toy. Comprehension of sex-typed connotations was predicted by home television viewing patterns but not by general knowledge of sex stereotypes.

726. Jackstadt, S.L., & Grootaert, C. (1980). Gender, gender stereotyping, and socioeconomic background as determinants of economic knowledge and learning. **Journal of Economic Education, 12**(1), 34-40.

Reports results of asking high school students who took the Test of Economic Understanding (TEU) (1) whether economics is a masculine or feminine topic and (2) whether they preferred male or female teachers in their social studies classes. Findings show students who did not gender stereotype economics, and had no gender preference for their teacher, did better on the TEU.

* Johnson, C.S., & Greenbaum, G.R. (1980). Are boys disabled readers due to sex-role stereotyping? **Educational Leadership.** (Cited as entry 280.)

727. Kaiser, S., et al. (1985). The role of clothing in sex-role socialization: person perceptions versus overt behavior. **Child Study Journal, 15**(2), 83-97.

Explores the role of clothing in sex-role socialization by comparing stereotypic clothing-play cognitions with overt play behavior relative to dress.

728. Kelly, A. (1988). Sex stereotypes and school science: a three year follow-up. **Educational Studies, 14**(2), 151-63.

Presents results of a follow-up to the Girls into Science and Technology Project and examines development over three-year period of children's sex stereotypes and their attitudes toward and achievements in science. Concludes that sex stereotypes are only weakly related to children's achievements in, choice of, and attitudes toward science. Results are shown as more salient for girls than boys.

729. Kingston, A.J., & Lovelace, T.L. (1979). First graders' perceptions of stereotyped story characters. **Reading**

Improvement, 16(1), 66-70.

Examines drawings made by first grade children after they had been read stories in which protagonists were presented in the first person. Concludes that children perceive males as being larger than females and that sex role stereotypes develop prior to school entrance.

730. Kleinke, C.L., & Nicholson, T.A. (1979). Black and white children's awareness of de facto race and sex differences. **Developmental Psychology, 15**(1), 84-86.

Reports results of picture-rating study showing black and white third-, fourth-, and fifth-grade children aware of de facto race and sex differences in American society.

* Koblinsky, S.A., & Cruse, D.F. (1981). The role of frameworks in children's retention of sex-related story content. **Journal of Experimental Child Psychology.** (Cited as entry 94.)

731. Kourilsky, M., & Campbell, M. (1984). Sex differences in a simulated classroom economy: children's beliefs about entrepreneurship. **Sex Roles: A Journal of Research, 10**(1-2), 53-66.

Study of "Mini-Society," an experience-based economics instructional program enrolling children in grades three through six. Measures participants' perceptions of entrepreneurship, occupational stereotyping, and sex differences in risk-taking, persistence, and economic success. During the program, no sex differences occurred in the latter three areas, and sex, occupational, and entrepreneurial stereotyping decreased after it.

732. Liben, L.S., & Signorella, M.L. (1980). Gender-related schemata and constructive memory in children. **Child Development, 51**(1), 11-18.

Reports results of a study in which first and second graders were (1) shown pictures of people in various traditional, nontraditional, and neutral occupations and activities, and (2) tested for recognition memory to examine relationship between children's gender attitudes and memories.

733. Leuptow, L.B. (1980). Social structure, social change and parental influence in adolescent sex-role socialization: 1964-1975. **Journal of Marriage and the Family, 42**(1), 93-103.

Results of this study of Wisconsin high school seniors were consistent with explanations involving role processes and structural effects. Same-sex influence appeared. Father's influence was related to instrumental orientations in boys. Contrary to expectations, there was no evidence of changing sex roles in the patterns of influence between 1964 and 1975.

* List, J.A., et al. (1983). Comprehension and inferences from traditional and nontraditional sex-role portrayals on television. **Child Development.** (Cited as entry 760.)

* Martin, S., & Cowles, M. (1983). Locus of control among children in various educational environments. **Perceptual and Motor Skills.** (Cited as entry 671.)

* Massad, C.M. (1981). Sex role identity and adjustment during adolescence. **Child Development.** (Cited as entry 672.)

734. Moore, H.A. (1988). Effects of gender, ethnicity, and school equity on students' leadership behaviors in a group game. **Elementary School Journal, 88**(5), 515-27.

Examines leadership skills and perception of leadership by students and teachers in desegregated elementary schools divided into high equity and low equity groups. In low equity schools, perceptions of leadership are reported lower among Hispanics than Anglos.

735. Nowicki, S., Jr. (1979). Sex differences in independence-training practices as a function of locus of control orientation. **Journal of Genetic Psychology, 135**(2), 301-02.
Investigates sex differences in independence-training practices

as a function of locus of control orientation for twelve-year olds.

736. Parsons, J.E. (1982). Sex differences in attributions and learned helplessness. **Sex Roles: A Journal of Research, 8**(4), 421-32.

Reports results of a study in which over 300 students assessed their causal attributions and expectations for success and failure in mathematics as well as their self concepts of math ability. Results varied, depending on research method employed, but did not when taken together support the hypothesis that girls are more learned helpless in mathematics than are boys.

737. Perry, D.G., & Bussey, K. (1979). The social learning theory of sex differences: imitation is alive and well. **Journal of Personality and Social Psychology, 37**(10), 1699-712.

Presents a modified social learning theory account of the contribution of imitation to sex role development.

* Phifer, S.J., & Plake, B.S. (1983). The factorial validity of the Bias in Attitude Survey scale. **Educational and Psychological Measurement.** (Cited as entry 779.)

738. Potkay, C.R., & Potkay, C.E. (1984). Perceptions of female and male comic strip characters II: favorability and identification are different dimensions. **Sex Roles: A Journal of Research, 10**(1-2), 119-28.

Reports results of a study of identification ratings of 20 comic strip characters replicating prediction male characters would elicit greater identification, even though previous research showed that female characters are seen in an equivalent or more favorable light than male characters. Significant interaction findings affirm a great degree of same sex identification.

739. Reis, S.M., & Callahan, C.M. (1989). Gifted females: they've come a long way--or have they? **Journal for the Education of the Gifted, 12**(2), 99-117.

Reviews research studies regarding sex differences, pointing out promising research directions, and discussing sex bias in programs and curriculum.

740. Richmond, P.G. (1984). An aspect of sex-role identification with a sample of twelve year olds and sixteen year olds. **Sex Roles: A Journal of Research, 11**(11-12), 1021-32.

Study of sex-role identification partly confirmed two hypotheses: (1) the social relationships of late childhood have attributes which encourage the feminine stereotype rather than the masculine stereotype; and (2) children of both sexes who attest to masculine characteristics feel higher levels of discordance than those who attest to female characteristics.

741. Ruch, L.O. (1984). Dimensionality of the Bem Sex Role Inventory: a multidimensional analysis. **Sex Roles: A Journal of Research, 10**(1-2), 99-117.

Replicates Pedhazur and Tetenbaum's study raising questions about the unidimensionality of feminine and masculine subscales of Bem Sex Role Inventory (BSRI). Factor analysis and smallest space analysis indicates subsets are not unidimensional.

742. Rybash, J.M., et al. (1979). The role of affect in children's attribution of intentionality and dispensation of punishment. **Child Development, 50**(4), 1217-30.

Examines role of affect in children's attribution of intentionality and dispensation of punishment. Sex differences are discussed.

743. Saltiel, J. (1982). Sex differences in occupational significant others and their role relationships to students. **Rural Sociology, 47**(1), 129-46.

Reports results of a study showing role relationships of others to 142 rural Montana high school students varies across socioeconomic status, residence, and level of aspiration for males, but not females.

* Scott, K.P., & Feldman-Summers, S. (1979). Children's reactions to textbook stories in which females are portrayed in traditionally male roles. **Journal of Educational Psychology.** (Cited as entry 307.)

744. Scott-Jones, D., & Clark, M. (1986). The school experiences of black girls: the interaction of gender, race and socio-economic status. **Phi Delta Kappan, 86**(7), 520-526.

Reviews available research on achievement of black females in science, mathematics, and verbal skills, concluding that black males enjoy a 'male advantage' over black females and that attending to inequities caused by race and social class is at least as important for black females as attending to inequities resulting from sex bias.

745. Serbin, L.A., & Sprafkin, C. (1986). The salience of gender and the process of sex typing in three-to-seven-year-old children. **Child Development, 57**(5), 1188-99.

Describes two measures of gender salience, one assessing the use of the gender dimension in classifying new information and the other assessing its use in making affiliation choices. Also examines the developmental course of gender salience from age three to age seven and the relation between salience and sex-role development.

* Shover, N., et al. (1979). Gender roles and delinquency. **Social Forces.** (Cited as entry 217.)

746. Sidelnick, D.J. (1987). Political attitudes of secondary school students: effects of grade, gender, and ability. **Journal of Social Studies Research, 11**(1), 7-14.

Investigates influence of gender, ability, and grade level on the political attitudes of ninth and twelfth grade students. Conclusions show (1) low ability subjects are less likely to support fundamental freedoms, and (2) females have greater respect for law and law officials.

747. Signorella, M.L. (1987). Gender schemata: individual differences and context effects. **New Directions, 38**, 23-37.

Reports results of a study supporting position that although individual differences have often been ignored, children differ in stereotyping of their gender schemata (identities and attitudes). Argues that children with traditionally stereotyped gender schemata process gender information differently from children who have less stereotyped schemata.

748. Signorella, M.L., & Liben, L.S. (1984). Recall and reconstruction of gender-related pictures: effects of attitude, task difficulty, and age. **Child Development, 55**(2), 393-405.

Reports results of a study testing two implications of Bartlett's constructive theory of memory (better memory for schema-consistent material and alteration of schema-inconsistent material).

* Silvern, L.E., & Katz, P.A. (1986). Gender roles and adjustment in elementary-school children: a multidimensional approach. **Sex Roles: A Journal of Research.** (Cited as entry 690.)

749. Simmons, B. (1980). Sex role expectations of classroom teachers. **Education, 100**(3), 249-53.

Reports results of a survey of elementary school teachers' and student teachers' expectations for boys and girls. Citing cultural factors as causes, both groups expected boys to be more aggressive and physically adept than girls. Girls were expected to be more emotional, intuitive, empathetic, and ambitious, due to biological factors.

750. Smith, J., & Russell, O. (1984). Why do males and females differ? Children's beliefs about sex differences. **Sex Roles: A Journal of Research, 11**(11-12), 1111-20.

Investigates relationship of children's beliefs about sex differences to their own age and gender. Children (seven, 10, and 15 year olds) were asked to explain their beliefs. Younger children's responses displayed a biological orientation, and older children a societal orientation. No evidence supported a hypothesized third stage of psychological orientation. Sex differences are discussed.

751. Smith, K.E. (1981). Male teachers in early childhood education: sex-role perceptions. **Humanist Educator, 20**(2), 58-64.

Assesses male preschool teachers' self-perceptions and sex-role perceptions of self and others. Male and female teachers in preschool and high school education were administered the Bem Sex Role Inventory and a repertory grid. Results indicate preschool male and female teachers were similar in levels of androgyny.

752. Steelman, L.C., & Powell, B. (1985). The social and academic consequences of birth order: real, artifactual, or both? **Journal of Marriage and the Family, 47**(1), 117-24.

Examines impact of birth order on social skills and academic performance of children and adolescents. Results reveal no significant relationship between birth order and academic performance but do reveal a significant positive relationship between birth order and social skills. Leadership skills were related to birth order for males.

* Trepanier-Street, M.L., & Romatowski, J.A. (1986). Sex and age differences in children's creative writing. **Journal of Humanistic Education and Development.** (Cited as entry 320.)

753. Tryon, B.W. (1980). Beliefs about male and female competence held by kindergartners and second graders. **Sex Roles: A Journal of Research, 6**(1), 85-97.

Investigates beliefs held by kindergartners and second graders regarding competence of boys and girls. Findings support previous reports that the sex-role stereotypic socialization process begins early and that the learning increases with age.

754. Wehren, A., & De Lisi, R. (1983). The development of gender understanding: judgments and explanations. **Child Development, 54**(6), 1568-78.

Data from boys and girls ages three, five, seven, and nine were collected on gender constancy judgments and explanations for correct, incorrect, and ambiguous judgments. Results verify acquisition of understanding of gender stability prior to gender constancy and support the shift with age from no constancy to pseudoconstancy to true constancy.

755. Weis, L. (1987). The 1980s: de-industrialization and change in white working class male and female youth cultural forms. **Metropolitan Education, 5,** 82-117. Special issue on The Future of City Schools.

Reports results of interviews revealing following attitudes of working class high school students: (1) boys resent institutional authority, view school in utilitarian terms, affirm patriarchy, and evidence racism; (2) girls emphasize the centrality of the private and marginalize the public, a wage labor identity and independence, and downplay a home-family identity.

Television

756. Eisenstock, B. (1984). Sex-role differences in children's identification with counterstereotypical televised portrayals. **Sex Roles: A Journal of Research, 10**(5-6), 417-30.

Reports results of a study of television's effectiveness in promoting nonsexist role learning. Finding show that androgynous preadolescent children are as likely as feminine children, and more likely than masculine ones, to identify with nontraditional televised models.

757. Field, D.E., & Anderson, D.R. (1985). Instruction and modality effects on children's television attention and comprehension. **Journal of Educational Psychology, 77**(1), 91-100.

Examines five- and nine-year olds' television viewing and program recall in response to learning instructions. Instructions affected visual-emphasis program segments only; visual orientation and cued recall increased in younger children; and free recall and cued recall were enhanced in older children. Sex differences are discussed.

758. Freeley, J.T. (1982). Content interests and media preferences of middle-graders: differences in a decade. **Reading World, 22**(1), 11-16.

Reports results of a study replicating work of early 1970s concerning media preferences and reading interests of intermediate grade children. Findings show reading interests of boys remained much the same, with those of girls changing. Both groups are reported to continue to prefer television over print media.

759. Goldsmith, E. (1987). Differences in reciprocal peer social relations among children who view low, moderate, and high amounts of television. **Home Economics Research Journal, 15**(4), 207-14.

Examines differences in reciprocal social relations related to low, moderate, and high quantities of television viewing. Children who viewed moderate amounts of television scored significantly higher than their peers. Sex differences are discussed.

760. List, J.A., et al. (1983). Comprehension and inferences from traditional and nontraditional sex-role portrayals on television. **Child Development, 54**(6), 1579-87.

Assesses third-grade children's comprehension of traditional and non-traditional female sex-role portrayals in television programs. For both programs, children demonstrated accurate memory for role-relevant information, but children with higher levels of sex-role stereotyping remembered less role-relevant information than did children with lower levels of stereotyping.

761. Morgan, M., & Rothschild, N. (1983). Impact of the new television technology: cable TV, peers, and sex-role cultivation in the electronic environment. **Youth & Society, 15**(1), 33-50.

Examines the intervening and/or conditioning roles of integration into peer groups (a traditional socializing agent) and access to new video technology via home cable viewing (a new socializing agent) in the relationship between television viewing and adolescents' sex-role images.

762. Mulac, A., et al. (1985). Male/female language differences and attributional consequences in children's television. **Human Communication Research, 11**(4), 481-506.

Findings of this study indicate that language of characters from children's television programs, both educational and commercial, is clearly gender differentiated, producing attributions that are consistent with sex-role stereotypes.

763. Peterson, G.W., & Peters, D.F. (1983). Adolescents' construction of social reality: the impact of television and peers. **Youth and Society**, **15**(1), 67-85.

Draws upon ideas about "television effects" and the adolescent peer group to illustrate how interconnections between these two socializing agents contribute to the adolescent's "construction of social reality." Examines how gender, sexual, consumer, and occupational roles as enacted by teenagers are a product of media and peer group influences.

764. Zillman, D., et al. (1980). Acquisition of information from educational television programs as a function of differently paced humorous inserts. **Journal of Educational Psychology**, **72**(2), 170-80.

Reports results of a study in which children viewed a television segment including humorous or non-humorous inserts paced either at slow or fast intervals or in uninterrupted fashion. Both humorous conditions produced information acquisition results that were superior to any of the non-humor situations. Sex differences are discussed.

Testing | Tests

765. Benson, J., et al. (1986). Effects of test-wiseness training and ethnicity on achievement of third- and fifth-grade students. **Measurement and evaluation in Counseling and Development, 18**(4), 154-62.

Reports results of a study to determine whether test-wiseness training would influence the achievement of students in math and reading. Significant effects are reported in math for fifth-grade students. Race effects favored white students. Sex differences are discussed.

766. Burton, S.A., & Goggin, W.C. (1984). FIRO-BC normative and psychometric data on 9- through 13-year-old children. **Journal of Clinical Psychology, 40**(3), 760-72.

Reports results of a study addressing the need to provide normative and psychometric data for the FIRO-BC questionnaire. Reports means, standard deviations, test-retest reliability coefficients, and interscale correlation coefficients. Data are reported separately for boys and girls.

767. Chase, C.I. (1986). Essay test scoring: interaction of relevant variables. **Journal of Educational Measurement, 23**(1), 33-41.

Reports results of a study testing the hypothesis that readers of an essay respond to a variable in terms of its context with other variables. Sex, race, reader expectation, and quality of handwriting were crossed to study their interaction effects. Results show complex interactions of expectations, writing, and sex within race.

768. Ekstrom, R.B., et al. (1979). Sex differences and sex bias in test content. **Educational Horizons, 58**(1), 47-52.

Reports results of content analyses for sex bias conducted on items from three widely-used achievement tests which together span the grade levels 1-12. A significant but modest correlation was found between an item's content bias and performance on that item by male and female students.

769. Guida, F.V., & Ludlow, L.H. (1989). A cross-cultural study of test anxiety. **Journal of Cross-Cultural Psychology, 20**(2), 178-90.

Reports results of a study comparing relative test anxiety of urban seventh- and eighth-grade students in North America and Chile. Sex differences are discussed.

770. Hale, R.L., & Potok, A.A. (1981). Sexual bias in the Slosson Intelligence Test. **Diagnostique, 6**(2), 3-7.

Results indicate that the SIT IQ predicts statistically distinct reading scores depending upon the sex of the child being evaluated. It is suggested that the bias needs to be considered in making psychological referrals about children. Derived regression equations for both boys and girls are provided.

* Harty, H., & Beall, D. (1984). Toward the development of a children's science curiosity measure. **Journal of Research in Science Teaching**. (Cited as entry 595.)

771. Hembree, R. (1988). Correlates, causes, effects, and treatment of test anxiety. **Review of Educational Research, 58**(1), 47-77

A meta-analysis of results of 562 studies illustrating the nature, effect, and treatment of academic test anxiety (TA). Ability, gender, and school grade level are shown among factors affecting TA.

772. Karmos, A.H., & Karmos, J.S. (1984). Attitudes toward standardized achievement tests and their relation to achievement test performance. **Measurement and Evaluation in Counseling and Development, 17**(2), 56-66.

Examines the attitudes of students in grades 6 through 9 toward standardized achievement tests. Results show scores on the Stanford Achievement Test are significantly related to students' perceptions of individual effort, test importance, and the use schools make of test results. Sex differences are discussed.

773. Koh, T., et al. (1984). Cultural bias in WISC subtest items: a response to Judge Grady's suggestion in relation to the PASE case. **School Psychology Review, 13**(1), 89-94.

Several items from the Information and Comprehension subtests of the Wechsler Intelligence Scale for Children were cited by Judge Grady in his opinion in the PASE (Parents in Action in Special Education) case as being culturally biased against black children. Error analysis used in this study showed no significant "cultural" differences between white and black children. Sex differences are discussed.

774. Lambert, N.M. (1986). Evidence on age and ethnic status bias in factor scores and the comparison score for the AAMD Adaptive Behavior Scale-School Edition. **Journal of School Psychology, 24**(2), 143-53.

Analyzes the contribution of gender, ethnic status, age, and school classification to the five factor scores and the comparison score of the Adaptive Behavior Scale-School Edition (ABS-SE). Results provide evidence for the validity of the ABS-SE factor and comparison scores and show the factor and comparison scores are not affected by gender or ethnic status.

775. Moe, K.C., & Johnson, M.F. (1988). Participants' reactions to computerized testing. **Journal of Educational Computing Research, 4**(1), 79-86.

Describes study of secondary school students (1) investigating their reactions to computerized testing, and (2) assessing practicability of this testing method in the classroom. Sex differences are discussed.

* Nagle, R.J. (1979). The predictive validity of the Metropolitan Readiness Tests, 1976 edition. **Educational and Psychological Measurement.** (Cited as entry 290.)

776. Newton, R.R. (1984). Maximum likelihood estimation of factor structures of anxiety measures: a multiple group comparison. **Educational and Psychological Measurement, 44**(2), 179-93.

Examines the construct generality of five self-report measures of anxiety across male and female samples, and illustrates the use of confirmatory maximum likelihood techniques for examining factorial invariance.

777. Nickel, E.J., et al. (1986). The New MAACL Scales with Adolescents: preliminary reliability and validity determinations. **Adolescence, 21**(81), 81-86.

Reports the reliability and concurrent validity of both the trait and state forms of the Multiple Affect Adjective Check List (MAACL) with a high school population. Findings indicate MAACL is sufficiently reliable and valid to warrant additional use with an adolescent population. Sex differences are discussed.

778. Obrzut, J.E., et al. (1981). An investigation of the DIAL as a pre-kindergarten screening instrument. **Educational and Psychological Measurement, 41**(4), 1231-41.

Reports results of a study of the validity of the Developmental Indicators for the Assessment of Learning (DIAL). Fifty-three kindergartners took the DIAL before school entrance and then had their Slosson Intelligence Test scores and Metropolitan Readiness Tests monitored for the school year. Sex differences are discussed.

* Peeler, E., & Rimmer, S.M. (1981). The assertiveness scale for

children. **Elementary School Guidance and Counseling.** (Cited as entry 474.)

779. Phifer, S.J., & Plake, B.S. (1983). The factorial validity of the Bias in Attitude Survey scale. **Educational and Psychological Measurement, 43**(3), 887-91.

Results of this Bias in Attitudes Survey (BIAS) suggest that the BIAS in relation to other sex-role scales is measuring more complete and complex attitudes toward sex roles.

780. Plake, B.S., et al. (1983). Differential performance of males and females on easy to hard item arrangements: influence of feedback at the item level. **Educational and Psychological Measurement, 43**(4), 1067-75.

Reports results of a study to investigate the effect of differential item performance by males and females on tests which have different item arrangements. Study allows for a more accurate evaluation of whether differential sensitivity to reinforcement strategies is a factor in performance discrepancies for males and females.

781. Plake, B.S., & Ansorge, C.J. (1984). Effects of item arrangement, sex of the subject, and test anxiety on cognitive and self-perception scores in a nonquantitative content area. **Educational and Psychological Measurement, 44**(2), 423-30.

Reports analysis of scores representing number of items right and self-perceptions for a nonquantitative examination assembled into three forms. Multivariate ANCOVA revealed no significant effects for the cognitive measure. However, significant sex and sex order effects are reported for perceptions scores not parallel to those reported previously.

* Plake, B.S., et al. (1981). Sex differences in mathematics components of the Iowa Tests of Basic Skills. **Psychology of Women Quarterly.** (Cited as entry 366.)

782. Plass, J.A., & Hill, K.T. (1986). Children's achievement strategies and test performance: the role of time pressure, evaluation anxiety, and sex. **Developmental Psychology, 22**(1), 31-36.

Examines how test anxiety affects children in certain evaluation situations and focuses on developing more valid and effective measurement procedures in school achievement testings. Third and fourth graders were divided into three anxiety groups and tested under time and no time pressures. Anxiety level, time pressure, and sex affected performance.

783. Purvis, M.A., & Bolen, L.M. (1984). Factor structure of the McCarthy Scales for males and females. **Journal of Clinical Psychology, 40**(1), 108-14.

Determines factor structure of the McCarthy Scales for referred rural children. Three meaningful factors emerged: verbal, perceptual, and motor factors for males and females. Results suggest McCarthy Scales reflect a general dimension of cognitive ability rather than distinct abilities.

* Reynolds, C.R. (1979). The invariance of the factorial validity of the Metropolitan Readiness Tests for blacks, whites, males, and females. **Educational and Psychological Measurement.** (Cited as entry 299.)

784. Reynolds, C.R., & Harding, R.E. (1983). Outcome in two large sample studies of factorial similarity under six methods of comparison. **Educational and Psychological Measurement, 43**(3), 723-28.

Compares six methods of measuring factorial similarity with regard to outcome based on two large data sets, one for an intelligence test and the other for a personality test. All indexes yielded comparable results. Comparing factors determined at random, all indexes yielded comparable results leading to a conclusion of dissimilarity. Sex differences are discussed.

785. Reynolds, C.R., et al.(1984). Between age and raw score increases on the Kaufman Assessment Battery for Children. **Psychology in the Schools, 21**(1), 19-24.

Explores relationship between age and intelligence test performance across race and evaluates developmental progression of scores and construct validity of the Kaufman Assessment Battery for Children. No significant race or sex differences are reported, supporting the validity of the K-ABC.

786. Silverstein, A.B., et al. (1983). Sex differences and sex bias on the Boehm Test of Basic Concepts: do they exist? **Psychology in the Schools, 20**(3), 269-70.

Reports results of administering form A of the Boehm Test of Basic Concepts (BTBC) to kindergartners. Neither mean scores nor standard deviations differed significantly, and boys and girls had identical score distributions. Internal criteria for bias yielded totally negative results, showing no evidence of sex differences or sex bias.

787. Skinner, N.F. (1983). Switching answers on multiple-choice questions: shrewdness or shibboleth? **Teaching of Psychology, 10**(4), 220-22.

Because of a belief that the alternatives they had chosen initially were probably correct, most subjects in this study were reluctant to change answers, and, consequently, did so only when they were highly confident in the change. Results show that more than half the changes were correct. Sex differences are discussed.

Toys | Play | Games

788. Barnett, T. (1986). An investigation of the significance of personality factors to individual children's perceptions of simulations and games. **Simulation/Games for Learning, 16**(1), 12-16.

Describes a study of children's perceptions of educational games and simulations to determine correlations between individual personality dimensions (psychoticism, extroversion, neuroticism) and pupils' perceptions of enjoyment and learning. Data were also grouped into personality clusters comparing data on perceived enjoyment and learning of geography simulations and games.

789. Blakemore, J.E.O., et al. (1979). Sex-appropriate toy preference and the ability to conceptualize toys as sex-role related. **Developmental Psychology, 15**(3), 339-40.

Reports results of two studies examining relation between identifying toys as "boys" or "girls" and sex-appropriate toy preferences.

790. Budd, B.E., et al. Spatial configurations: Erickson reexamined. **Sex Roles: A Journal of Research, 12**(5-6), 571-77.

Erickson's 1951 study of gender differences in preadolescents' play construction was replicated and expanded to correct for sex bias of materials. Erickson's finding of innate biological differences in the experience and perception of space was not confirmed. Instead, differences were attributed to the materials provided.

791. Cole, D., & LaVoie, J.C. (1985). Fantasy play and related cognitive development in 2- to 6-year-olds. **Developmental Psychology, 21**(2), 233-240.

Examines developmental changes in specific types of fantasy play and the relation of role taking, egocentrism, and receptive vocabulary in two- to six-year-olds. Both frequency and duration of material and ideational fantasy play increased with age, but play patterns differed. Data suggest developmental progression from object to person fantasy play does not occur. Sex differences are discussed.

792. Eisenberg, N., et al. (1982). Children's reasoning regarding sex-typed toy choices. **Child Development, 53**(1), 81-86.

The purposes of this study were (1) to explore the meaning of children's choices in toy preference tasks, and (2) to determine if children's understanding of sex appropriateness of toys is an important conscious determinant of sex-typed object choices.

793. Pellegrini, A.D., & Perlmutter, J.C. (1989). Classroom contextual effects on children's play. **Developmental Psychology, 25**(2), 289-96.

Reports results of three studies suggesting children's play was mediated by their age, playmates' sex, and play props. Children's behavior seemed to change with age and with the children's consideration of the sex-role appropriateness of interacting in particular play areas and with particular peers.

* Rogers, M., et al. (1981). Cooperative games as an intervention to promote cross-racial acceptance. **American Educational Research Journal.** (Cited as entry 522.)

794. Tauber, Margaret A. (1979). Parental socialization techniques and sex differences in children's play. **Child Development, 50**(1), 225-34.

Reports results of a study in which (1) videotapes were made of children, aged eight and nine, playing alone and playing with a parent in a toy room, and (2) data on parents' work histories, socialization techniques, and self report of sex roles in relation to children's play activities were analyzed. Effects of family constellation are investigated.

795. Wolfgang, C.H. (1983). A study of play as a predictor of social-emotional development. **Early Child Development and Care, 13**(1), 33-54.

Investigates whether the Piagetian forms of sensorimotor, symbolic, and constructional play--together with controlled demographics such as socioeconomic status, age, and sex--predict social-emotional variables on the Devereux Child Behavior Rating Scale.

AUTHOR INDEX

Numbers refer to bibliographic entries.

SUBJECT INDEX

Numbers refer to bibliographic entries.

Categories, as listed in the Contents, are set off in bold type, alphabetically.

All entries assume relation to the title: *Sex Differences and Education.*